How The Earth Saved My Soul

Nature Based Healing And Wisdom

By Travis Bodick

Copyright 2016

SoulRemedy.org

Table of Contents:

For My Wife Tasha ~

Whenever I am lost you are always my medicine <3

"The best remedy for those who are afraid, lonely or unhappy is to go outside, somewhere where they can be quite alone with the heavens, nature and God. Because only then does one feel that all is as it should be and that God wishes to see people happy, amidst the simple beauty of nature. As longs as this exists, and it certainly always will, I know that then there will always be comfort for every sorrow, whatever the circumstances may be. And I firmly believe that nature brings solace in all troubles."

— Anne Frank, The Diary of a Young Girl

Nature is Medicine for the Soul

"Man's heart away from nature becomes hard." ~ Standing Bear

I was in the forest with my wife and a new friend. All around us, all I could see was sacred medicine – the plants, the trees, the rocks. The sun and the moon. The call of a crow and the knock of a woodpecker. So simple, yet so often ignored by everyone else in the city where we lived – this wilderness was surrounded by the hustle and bustle of modern city life, but we had found heart and calm lying in the forest just outside the reach of car horns and blinking lights of the town. The stress of life and constant productivity melted away and our hearts started to speak with whispers when we entered the forest.

That day a special spirit gifted me with an idea – and that is when this book started. Nature based rituals to help you connect with your own heart, with nature and community, with spirit, and with your primal nature. The world all around us has its own medicine for us to tap into for healing our body, mind and soul - and the world shares this with you gladly.

There is no wrong or right way to connect to nature – it is there as a gift to all of us. It feeds us, gives us air and life, and is the easiest doorway into connection with your own Spirit and to experience God's wonder in your own life. When we live close to nature, divinity and Spirit is all around us, and with this book I hope to inspire others to reconnect with their primal nature and bring that nature into their own lives for healing and inspiration. For me, nature is the truest medicine I have ever found, and I am honored and grateful for the opportunity to share this gift of medicine with all.

There are many ways to connect more deeply with nature and grow in deeper relationship to yourself and to Spirit. I hope you have the opportunity to experience many of them. My hope is that readers of this book will make the information here their own and be inspired to find their own path and own connection to nature – this book is just one possible starting point for your journey, or another tool to deepen the journey you already are on. There is no wrong or right here and no dogma – just you and nature. Follow your heart and you will always find love.

The Earth is Your Birthright

There are many different ways to connect with nature and many different ways to work with this book. I am trying to offer here multiple different choices, possibilities and paths so that people can find what resonates with them. The uniting feature is that all these rituals are based on connecting with yourself to find healing and guidance from the Earth and that all the rituals in this book come from my personal practice of what has helped me in my life.

Some of these rituals and practices I discovered myself through inspiration. Some were taught to me by specific people or from specific lineages or cultures. Others are practices which seem common to many different peoples and cultures. When the ceremony or philosophy comes from a specific source I will try to mention the source. I am sharing here my personal story and personal practice – it is an eclectic practice derived from many sources so it will have familiar pieces to some, but I can only share what I know. I studied and tested many ideas and methods in the creation of this practice and it is always growing and evolving each year... This book is very personal to me and with it I hope to give you an inside peak into the life and practice of a nature based healer.

Most of these rituals can be performed just with your own body, the land around you, or rocks and plants you can gather straight from the Earth. A few may need some minimal supplies but most do not. Even though this is my personal practice, I do not share this information for others to copy me – my hope is to inspire so that you can more easily create your own personal practice. These exercises can be integrated into just about any tradition, and you can also alter them or fine-tune them to fit your own preference. Be creative!

Many of these practices might be called shamanic practices, or witchcraft or pagan or any other number of different names…. I think of these practices as spiritual in nature, but there is a psychological and emotional component as well. Some people might claim it is all psychological, and while I would disagree, I think it is a valid view for people who do not believe in spirits. Whichever way you view it the results are the same – these practices will help you relieve stress, help you know yourself more deeply, and help you heal or find guidance if that is what you seek. Your body has incredible power to heal itself – you just need to know how to access that power!

Anyone anywhere on the planet can benefit from these practices. Earth Medicine is your birthright as a child of this planet. This book is not the medicine – Mother Earth herself is, and this book is just a guide for getting to know her a little better.

We Are All Nature

"Forget not that the earth delights to feel your bare feet and the winds long to play with your hair." ~ Khalil Gibran

Modern culture teaches us to fear nature. We live indoors where there is an illusion of control and we see ourselves as somehow separate or above nature. We forget what we are and where we came from – the Earth. We are her children. This disconnect from nature and our primal selves results in so much pain and illness – the way we pollute the earth is a macrocosmic example of how we treat our bodies and our minds on a daily basis. The disconnect results in many psychological, spiritual and even physical problems – because we are living in an illusion. There is no real way to separate yourself from nature or your own essence – truth is we depend on Mother Nature and that scares us! Our very survival depends on how we connect with and care for her. Clearly we need Mother Nature and cannot live without her!

When you describe something – whether that is a state, feeling, relationship, experience or anything else, "natural" almost always means good, right, easy or healthy. When we describe something as unnatural it often means it is disconnected or out of sync in some way – something is off or imbalanced. Deep in our hearts true wisdom still exists and each of us has the knowing of who we are – even if our brains temporarily forget. There is a desire to be natural – close to nature, like nature – like our true selves.

Nature doesn't just provide food, shelter, medicine and water – it provides something else. It provides beauty and inspiration – food for the soul. Anywhere you look at the natural world, all the colors fit together perfectly. The shapes all create beauty. Nature never goes out of style!

And nature feeds our souls in other ways as well! When you walk in the forest the trees don't just exchange breath with you – they also exchange their energy. Ancient mystical traditions knew this, and recently science has started to discover the same thing! Just spending time next to trees heals you – it helps you relax and relieve stress. The trees share their energy – their nectar if you will, and this energy is medicine. It is food for the soul.

But if we have lost our connection to nature in some ways, and if we have become confused about how nature relates to us – how can we remember to connect with and care for her responsibly again? Through science and through studying the cultures who still stay connected to the land and its beauty!

Science - noun - *the systematic study of the nature and behavior of the material and physical universe, based on observation, experiment, and measurement, and the formulation of laws to describe these facts in general terms. - Merriam Websters online dictionary*

This definition does not only describe how scientists can teach us to work with nature responsibly and ethically, but it also describes the practice of indigenous people over many thousands of years before our word "science" was ever invented. There is knowledge held by indigenous wisdom keepers and other people who live close to the land that luckily has survived to this day – and this wisdom can teach us so much about the world around us and our own "inner-nature" (the nature inside of us all).

The best part about this wisdom is that it isn't something that requires a teacher or blind faith in any way – it is something you can experience for yourself! It is all around you in the birds, the trees, the sky and the rocks! The whole earth is filled with energy and consciousness working together in reciprocation and a constant flux of shifting harmony and balance. The trick to connecting with this reciprocating flow in a more conscious way is heavily based on intention to do so as well as openness and willingness to embrace new perspectives, ideas and ways of living.

Study nature. Study yourself. Know your heart and express your heart. Celebrate the world around you. Sit with intention and hear the Earth speak her wisdom.

All Life Comes From Water

"One thorn of Experience is worth a whole wilderness of warning." ~ James Russel Lowell

I grew up in a broken home. My parents separated when I was 3 years old and I was constantly going back and forth between their homes. In our modern world it is common for many children to grow up this way – I don't know how much it effects everyone else, but it wouldn't surprise me to find that it was as hard for them as it was for me – it affected me greatly in all areas of my life. My father's side of the family was Jewish but he himself had no religious upbringing and didn't seem to think much about God or anything spiritual. His only concern was being a good person and this is what he taught me. My mother's side of the family was Catholic originally but while I was growing up she went through a number of different Christian churches as we moved from city to city. She often took me to church when I visited her and would make us read Bible stories together, but honestly – I always hated it. Even as a child the Bible and its stories never made sense to me and church seemed more like brainwashing than anything else.

A few times though I did feel something that confused me… An energy or a "spirit" that I couldn't explain. At church they claimed this was the Holy Spirit, but I never really believed them because most of what they said was contradictory nonsense. God preaching peace and then ordering his followers to start wars, or claiming unconditional love then sending people who never heard of Christ to Hell… If a small child could so easily see through their stories I wondered why all these adults bought into it so easily. Maybe they just wanted security and hope and didn't know where else to look?

Since I had no other clues where to search I just explained away any feelings I had that seemed spiritual. It must just be my imagination or something I don't understand yet but has a totally reasonable scientific explanation. As I grew up I became more and more opposed to churches and religions because I saw how much harm was done in their name and I considered myself a staunch atheist. In school I even gave speeches and presentations on why it was illogical and impossible for any God or spirit to exist – some students even told me I made them question their own faith. I was good at rational arguments – not only in convincing others, but especially in convincing myself.

When I was 20 years old I was living on my own and working full time while in college part time. One day while walking in downtown Seattle with a close friend we saw a travel agency advertising tickets to Costa Rica at what seemed like a cheap price… So we both bought tickets right then on a whim. I could barely afford to travel at all but I was so excited – this would be my first real trip somewhere exotic on my own. No family to watch over me – just my friend and me for 3 weeks in the jungle and on the beaches. We didn't make a single plan for our trip till we got on the airplane and opened our guide book for the first time. I felt wild, adventurous, and free.

About a week into this trip I took a boogie board out into the ocean and started swimming out to catch some waves. If you have never been boogie boarding before, it involves a smaller version of a surf board which you lie down on your stomach instead of standing on – but you swim out and catch a wave which sends you back to shore. As I was swimming out waves would crash over my head and the board – these were smaller waves but for someone inexperienced like me they were big and powerful. Maybe about 5 feet high waves – and to me they were a bit scary because I could feel the intense power of the ocean behind those waves and just the day before I had been scuba diving with sharks nearby. I loved the feeling though – the open expanse of the ocean, the humility taught to me by the power of the waves, and the rush of speeding across the water. My board was pretty cheap and flimsy, but seemed good enough for a beginner. Sometimes I would get knocked off the board by a wave but there was a strap attaching the board to my ankle which always pulled me up to the surface and kept my board close by.

So there I was having the time of my life out in the ocean of Costa Rica – not knowing my life was about to change forever.

A large wave knocked me off of my board and pulled me under the water. Apparently my boogie board was too old and cheap because the safety strap on my ankle came off and the board left me. I felt this current sucking me down further into the ocean and I was disoriented – I couldn't see much under the water and I was spinning with the force of the waves. I was a great swimmer and in excellent shape though so I wasn't worried yet – I knew I could get back up to the surface and I would just have a long swim back to the shore if I couldn't find my board. A naive 20 year old, I always knew nothing would seriously harm me and I could never drown – stuff like that only happened to other people!

I underestimated the power of the ocean though. I was stuck in an undertow and it kept pulling me down to the oceans floor. My body kept twirling with the waves even as I tried to right myself and figure out which direction was up. Soon I was pushed into the sand on the ocean floor – I think I must have been about 30 feet below the surface. I tried to push myself off of the ocean floor so I could swim back up, but every time I pushed more waves would just pummel me across the sand and rocks twirling my body around like a rag doll. I felt so powerless because I couldn't even get an inch off of the ground. The waves were so strong it felt like I was getting kicked and punched from every direction at once while the rocks and sand kept coming up to hit me as I rolled over and over with the waves. As I struggled in the dark water fear started to creep in.

I had never felt so powerless in my life. And I was so confused – the force of the waves and my bodies spinning was knocking my brain around and I was so disoriented from rolling over and over myself. One second I was having fun riding waves and suddenly I was fighting for my life. I started to realize I was in real danger and I needed to do something. I thought frantically for any way out but I was alone under the ocean and no one even knew I was down there. I only had minutes of breath available to me and as the waves tumbled me over and over my time was quickly running out. I had never felt so hopeless before, and never felt so alone.

I fought frantically for my life and a deep fear came over me. I was getting weaker and weaker by the second – my arms and legs burned and my muscles started to feel like jelly. My lungs ached and my body started trying to gag – but if my mouth opened the ocean would rush in to fill my longs so I fought against the gagging of my body as well as the waves of the ocean now. My vision was starting to go dark around the edges and I was seeing stars before my eyes. My vision got darker and darker and I got weaker and weaker. For the first time in my life I thought I was truly powerless in every way and I was going to die here – there was nothing I could do about it.

It only took a moment to accept my death – there was no denying it. No fighting it. My life was over. And suddenly I thought to myself – maybe it didn't matter anyways. Life was full of suffering. Maybe I didn't need to suffer anymore. I didn't think I was going to heaven or going to any afterlife – I was an atheist and thought the end was just the end. But that seemed okay – an end to the suffering. A rest. I suddenly for the first time in my life admitted to myself that I was depressed. I had no dreams or real goals in my life – I was just going through the motions. Work, make money, spend it all on bills and be poor no matter how much you work, wishing I could be with women who had no interest in me, wishing I was important but feeling like I was just another nothing in a long line of people who didn't matter… I hated modern culture and felt like I couldn't relate to all the people living in denial about reality who thought money would buy them happiness. I never admitted to myself I was depressed before – I just thought everyone felt the way I did and it wasn't depression if the whole word was depressed right? Then it's just normal? Dying suddenly seemed like a gift – I could leave all the pain and suffering behind without the shame of suicide.

In that moment I gave up. I gave up because there was nothing else to do, but I also gave up because I wanted to. Death seemed easier. I stopped struggling for life and suddenly I felt this deep peace – a feeling I had never known before. As the feeling of peace and comfort and acceptance washed over me I experienced something strange – I left my body.

Suddenly I was no longer in the ocean and no longer aware of any body. I was racing through a tunnel like I had never seen before. At the end of the tunnel was light and as I entered into the light I became the light and all I knew was light for an eternal moment. Then I started to see things. I saw every single moment of my life in review – but it was like watching a movie and I saw everything different this time. I had the same thoughts and emotions, but behind those thoughts I was observing from a new perspective. Things I had never cared about before seemed more meaningful, and things that had seemed so important before didn't matter. I watched my whole life, and as I got back to the moment in the ocean my perspective shifted again. I saw my family without me there. I saw my funeral and all the people I loved missed me. My family. I suddenly realized that I wasn't just a person, but I was a part of something larger then myself. I knew these people more deeply and was suddenly aware that I was a part of something with them – in some strange way I even *was* them because together we were part of a greater whole. I felt so horrible for giving up and I wished that I could help them. I saw all these other people I never knew suffering and I wished I could help them as well. I felt their suffering and while I knew life had to include some suffering I also had this realization that by working together and loving each other we could ease our suffering in some ways. People could help each other, and living wasn't just for yourself – it was for everyone and everything.

I realized in that moment how many people had sacrificed so much so that I could have a life. Everyone that came before me sacrificed so that I could be born and live. And there were more to come after me. Life was eternal, but my moment in life was so short – maybe it wasn't such a burden to spend a few decades on this earth to be a part of this miracle called life. Maybe there was more to life then I had thought before, and maybe I had something I could offer to others – maybe we all had something to share together. I felt a sudden urge to honor my loved ones, honor the ancestors, and honor life itself – by living till my last breath and participating in this experience with creation.

I didnt realize it at the time, but that was the moment I decided to walk a spiritual path and become a healer. This insight and perspective would change the entire course of my life.

Suddenly I remembered myself and remembered my body in the ocean and I felt this tug... Things blurred as I felt something pulling me. I became aware of my body slowly and suddenly realized that there were hands under my armpits lifting me up – I wasn't kicking or swimming at all but being pulled to the surface of the ocean. I was heading towards a light again – but this time it was the light of the sun!

I broke the surface of the ocean and took one breath before another wave crashed over my head. I managed to stay close to the surface though and didn't get sucked back under. I had a second to look around as I took another breath – no one was around. Had I really felt hands carrying me up? I saw the shore but it was so far away. I was exhausted and weak and confused – I didn't know if I could make it back. I struggled to swim in my weakened state as the waves kept coming over the back of my head and temporarily pushing me back under or tossing me around. Somehow I made it back and climbed onto the shore again to lie down and catch my breath.

Shortly afterwards my friend who I was traveling with found me and asked where I had been – he had been searching for me for an hour he said and couldn't find me. I just told him I had been boogie boarding and he must have missed me – I said nothing about drowning. I was too confused to explain my experience, too ashamed to admit my depression, and too attached to my atheist worldview to admit I might have had a spiritual experience. In fact, the world had become scary in a way, as I felt that there may be a whole side of reality that I know nothing about. Realizing I knew nothing scared me like nothing else ever had – how could I live my life well or make any decisions with so much ignorance?

An Atheist Questions Himself

"I like it when a flower or a little tuft of grass grows through a crack in the concrete. It's so fuckin' heroic." ~ George Carlin

I enjoyed the rest of my trip in Costa Rica and when I got home I went back to life as usual. Back to work, back to school, back to hanging out with my friends. Something felt different – I was a little less sure about myself but I wouldn't admit it. I was trying to ignore what I had experienced in the ocean. I was an atheist and had no belief in any afterlife or any spirits – I thought that when you died that was that and nothing else happened. I told myself that I must have just been delirious in the ocean even though that explanation didn't really make sense to me... How had I gotten out of the undertow and back to the surface of the ocean? Why had I experienced all those weird visions and feelings? Why had it all felt so much more real then anything else I had ever experienced?

Mostly I didn't think about the experience at all, and for a while I didn't tell a single other person about it. I was too confused and was too arrogant to admit I didn't know how the world works or couldn't understand what I had experienced. I was also incredibly ashamed about my recently realized depression and ashamed I had given up so easily. How could I tell my family or friends that I hadn't even tried to save myself but had really wanted to die? In the ocean drowning seemed like a way to almost commit suicide without anyone having to know I committed suicide – the perfect escape... But I couldn't tell anyone about it now that I had survived. I was way too macho to talk about my feelings or my depression with anyone – so I just pretended everything was normal.

A few months later a couple friends asked if I wanted to eat magic mushrooms with them. I had never tried them before but it sounded exciting. I researched them a little bit online and found out that they were physically safe and not harmful to the body so I thought it sounded alright. I was a little scared of having a "bad trip" but my friends had tried the mushrooms before and said they were fine. Before then I had only ever smoked cannabis occasionally and tried something called Salvia Divinorum once so I basically didn't have any experience

18

with psychedelics but a couple of my friends were more experienced and they had gotten the mushrooms for us.

I was with 3 friends when we ate the mushrooms together. They went for a walk outside while I wanted to stay and listen to music in the house, so I had a little time by myself. While I was alone something strange and surprising happened – suddenly it felt like time had frozen and I felt in deep awe of this presence. I didn't believe in God but something inside me said this presence was God – this deep feeling of awe and wonder. I felt peace and ecstasy and love so deeply I couldn't even understand or relate to the feelings – they were so overwhelmingly intense it was otherworldly. I started crying – the feeling of this presence was so powerful and wonderful and confusing to me... I had a vision of me in the ocean again and I felt the hands under my arms again which had lifted me up to the surface. I heard a voice inside my head say "All life is connected. We are one. You are alive here to fulfill your purpose."

And as soon as I felt that message it was gone. It had felt like eternity that I was in that presence but I somehow knew it had been less than a second. I sat there for a while confused – I told myself I don't believe in God. But suddenly I wondered... Maybe there is more to reality and to life then I or anyone knows. Maybe I was wrong in my beliefs. I wondered if there was something out there I didn't know about – some invisible part of reality or God even... And if there was – I felt like I had to know about it, at least a little. How could I go through life ignoring a whole side of reality?

I didn't know at this point whether or not I believed in God anymore... But I decided to try and open my mind a little more and look into things. I decided to test my beliefs and test my reality to see what I could find. But I didn't really know how to do this... I knew at church they wouldn't really help me understand anything – they would just tell me a story and tell me to praise Jesus and give them money. I knew their story wasn't right – it had too many holes and contradictions still. I didn't want to believe anyone's story – I needed to experience things for myself to really know for certain. I didn't just want to believe – I wanted to know from experience. I had no clue how to do this – but the only place I knew to maybe start was with psychedelics just because of the recent experience I had had with the mushrooms.

So I started testing my reality and trying to open my mind with all kinds of psychedelics. I didn't really know what I was doing, but I was testing things out and trying to find a way. I suddenly became very excited about this project – I thought about it all the time and started to read about psychedelics online and in a couple books. Later on I would specifically feel called to work with natural plant medicines only but at the time I didn't know the difference between plant medicines and psychedelics and I had no clue that in some parts of the world people used plants and entheogens as part of a spiritual practice – I thought I was the only one with this "new" idea. I had only ever heard of drug abusers and hippies using psychedelics before and society told me they were all horrible criminals, artists, or rock stars... I thought I was the only person crazy enough to think psychedelics might teach me about God or reality.

I think a lot of other people might have been doing psychedelics at parties or something like that, but I wasn't going to many parties at this time, and I greatly preferred doing the psychedelics at home where I had privacy and space to focus on the experience. I had just a couple friends who were on the same page as me regarding these substances and often it would just be 2-3 of us taking psychedelics together. We all felt drawn to these mystical and insightful experiences that would happen when we took large doses and focused inwards – so we weren't talking or playing around a lot.... Mostly we would light a bunch of candles, set up a hookah and put on some good music – then do what we called "tripping out." If you just lied around and focused inward for long enough then eventually something would happen – you would leave your body or have deep insights about your life.

We didn't really know what we were doing, so this was all a guessing game based on trial and error and learning from our own experiences. One thing we discovered was that to go deeper and get the best results seeking the mystical experiences or personal insights – we had to find a way to make ourselves feel vulnerable and open. This was hard for a few guys in their early 20's hanging out

– we were not used to being vulnerable around other men. Society taught us to be macho, to keep up walls around our emotions, and to wear a mask. Being vulnerable was the opposite of all those things. So we really had to work against our programming here – against the bad habits society had taught us. I know now that there are better ways to do this, but at the time what worked for us in our ignorant applications of these substances was doing really large doses of psychedelics in a private and "safe" feeling environment. The environment was important because you couldn't distract yourself with thinking about impressing others or how you are supposed to behave in public. The large dose was important for helping us let go – because we didn't know how to meet these substances half way so we needed them to overpower us. We really needed them to break through our emotions, and in a way needed to almost scare ourselves with the intensity of the dose to help ourselves feel vulnerable. I would never work this way with these substances now, but at the time this is what worked for us and was the only way we knew.

To reach that difficult vulnerable goal of ours we took some really large doses of things like mushrooms or LSD. Sometimes we included MDMA or DMT or nitrous oxide. A few times I even ordered San Pedro cactus online and made us tea with it. We tried all kinds of substances because we wanted to find out what worked best and only knew how to search for this by trial and error. We often chose doses that we thought would push us to the edge of a bad trip – if we weren't a little bit scared it was hard to let down our walls and be vulnerable. We had so much programming about wearing masks and being men, that even with our best friends it was hard to be open and exposed. We would take such large doses that we couldn't resist the power of the substance on our consciousness anymore – it would flatten all resistance or effort to stay in control and we were forced to just let go and see where it took us. We were voyaging into our inner minds, and within ourselves we found the entire universe – and we found God.

Sometimes we would experience a total loss of knowing ourselves and lose the sense of experiencing ourselves as physical... Some call this ego loss. We would go so deep into our inner worlds that we would dissolve and become only energy. All we knew and experienced in this eternal moment was energy. Time would stop, and it would suddenly feel like you were one with infinity – one with everything. Like all that existed was the same energy expressing itself in different ways. I had never heard of this concept before but it started to change the way I viewed life and the world around me. I started to have understanding and compassion for others. I started to feel less alone – like no matter where I was, God was with me too. And in these moments of pure clarity and ego-death, I would have insights about myself and my life, and about what was really important to me. Priorities started shifting, and as they did, I found myself being more like myself (if that makes sense). Like I was uncovering my true self and learning how to express that instead of wearing the mask society had forced me to wear. As I took off the mask and was more real about who I was – I felt happier.

We were really pushing the edge here in order to get vulnerable and reveal ourselves to our own consciousness. The large doses of these substances were physically safe but still very scary – there was the risk of traumatizing ourselves emotionally and psychologically. You are extra sensitive in these altered states, so you have to be a little careful. But in finding our edge between a therapeutic and mystical dose and what some people called a "bad trip" was not always easy. Sometimes we really crossed the line and went overboard and had very difficult or scary experiences. Sometimes the psychedelics would get dark. But there was also something interesting in these darker or "bad trips" – in many cases they could be the most healing as long as no one got hurt or permanently traumatized.

We started to realize that "bad trips" weren't really bad – they were an encounter with your shadow side. These experiences seemed to be caused by repressed emotions coming to the surface to be looked at and learned from – but the repressed emotions were often so scary and uncomfortable that your first impulse was to run from them. Running would make it harder and possibly even traumatic – but if we faced our fears and worked through them we often learned incredible amounts about ourselves and would experience a healing of our inner wounds. Like letting go of emotional baggage and trauma by re-experiencing it from a new perspective. We adopted the motto "Know Thyself" because we felt like this was where all our healing and insights were coming from. We started thinking that maybe the "bad trips" were the best ones to have. Looking back on this, I would say that most bad trips are really an opportunity for healing, but that there is also a potential for trauma when there is no guide to help you work through it, so in some ways I think we were lucky things worked out as well as they did.

As I got further into this experimental healing and learning process it started to become more and more important to me... I was so depressed in my life, but suddenly I had found a way to treat that depression. I started to feel hopeful about the future. I didn't only feel better when I took the psychedelics – I felt better afterwards and I had more direction and purpose in my life. The benefits lasted well after the actual experience and effects from the substance. These altered states would show me ways that I treated other people poorly, and would show me ways to correct that behavior and be more compassionate. They would inspire deeper love inside of me for myself, my friends and family, and for the world around me. Sometimes I would lose my ego and become one with the entire universe – and I didn't feel so alone anymore within that oneness. I started to see God as this living energy and consciousness that existed within everything. The universe was one giant universal energy recycling itself as stars exploded then formed into planets where life could emerge, then the planets eventually fell apart to reform as new stars... We are stardust experiencing itself in this moment before we pass on and become something else like grass or worm food...

Since I didn't know where else to look for answers and guidance I felt that the psychedelics were my only source of knowledge and healing. This scared me since many psychedelics are illegal and it felt like there was a conspiracy to keep the truth from people. All of these safe mind-expanding substances were illegal for some reason, and all of society had been taught lies about them to the point where I would be viewed as a law breaking drug addict if I told anyone that mushrooms were healing my depression. I feared telling my friends and family. I feared living depressed forever if I stopped what I was doing. I also feared going down this path on my own, but it seemed to be the only way.

I had a number of what people call "bad trips," but I experienced them differently than many would expect... Most often they would produce disorientation and fear as my ego was ripped away from me. I was losing control and losing my sense of self and would resist the experience. But somewhere in the process I would find deep truths and learn important but difficult lessons about myself – and this would turn the "bad trip" into the most healing of all my experiences. I started to learn that the most difficult psychedelic experiences were often the most insightful and while I feared them, I also lusted after their knowledge and healing.

In retrospect, taking these large doses without any guidance was not the best way to learn about these medicines or to learn about spirituality because I had no clue what I was doing. I could have easily traumatized myself or even given myself PTSD. If I had known of any teacher that I resonated with and could learn under that would have been a much better option, but at this time in my life I was very limited. I had no clue that others worked with psychedelic medicines to find insight and connect with God and if I did know about it I wouldn't have known where to look for those teachers or communities on the same path. So I went into the unknown alone.

I kept testing things out and working with entheogens in an attempt to connect with the spirit world and learn more about reality and slowly I discovered a few friends with a somewhat similar perspective – people who also felt that psychedelics opened up the spiritual world for them or helped them heal and learn about themselves. A couple friends told me about trauma they had experienced as a child which had always haunted them – but somehow the psychedelics helped liberate them from the fetter of those memories. The fact that we could even tell anyone else about the past abuse was a huge sign of our healing because before it had always been a repressed and shameful secret. Now we were not only letting go of the past and the control it had had on us, but we were confident enough to be ourselves around others and to express even our darkest secrets without fear. Slowly we saw more and more progress and potential and we started to grow into more confident and happy people together.

I was also desperately trying to find signs from elsewhere that some other people might have had similar insights as ours. I started reading anything I could find on psychedelics and eventually also started branching off from there into reading about other spiritual practices like meditation, yoga and Kabbalah. I was especially interested in anything practice based and more mystical oriented – I didn't just want someone to tell me what to believe, but I wanted to experience it firsthand so that I could really know for myself.

The first book which really opened my mind was called Supernatural by Graham Hancock. This was a hefty book with lots of detailed research and the author also was somewhat experienced in working with entheogens as well – specifically a plant medicine called Ayahuasca. Over the course of about 2 months I read this book and I experienced something very strange. At this time I had started having visions – of course some of them were caused by the psychedelics but some of them I experienced while sober. I thought I was having what some people call "flashbacks" though these visions were always original and not repeats of something that had happened while altered from entheogens. Three times in a row I would have a vision that was totally new and confusing to me – like nothing I had ever heard of before, and then days later I would read about the same exact vision in Supernatural. This always happened where I had the vision before reading about it, and then the book would describe it perfectly just a few days later. I will share one of these experiences as an example.

I was with one other friend and we had eaten psilocybin mushrooms earlier in the day together. We were lying in a candle lit room and decided at this point to smoke DMT (dimethyltryptamine) followed by inhaling nitrous oxide (we called this the "DMT whip-it"). I smoked DMT from a special pipe and then laid down and closed my eyes while breathing in the nitrous. Suddenly I saw elves everywhere – not the regular elves you might think of but short tiny people with giant toothy grins and tiny arms and legs. There were a dozen or more of them and they started crawling all over me smiling at me – I had never seen that many spirits before and didn't know if they were real, but I could feel and see them and something about this particular vision seemed more real than reality. I had this feeling deep inside that something important or significant was going on but I couldn't explain why.

These little spirit people then picked me up and started carrying me above their heads towards and then into a tunnel. I opened my eyes and I could see the room I was physically in, but I could also see all the little elf people and I could see the tunnel transposed over the room itself as if I was in both at once. It was too disorienting with my eyes opened so I closed them again and watched as I was carried through the tunnel and then underwater to some sort of cave.

The little people laid my body down in the cave and then quickly began to remove all of my bones. I started to freak out for a second, but I think what kept me calm was my own disbelief in the situation... It felt and seemed so real, but there was also a part of me that thought "Oh, I must just be imagining the whole thing because I'm in an altered state." I didn't know how to stop the process anyways and my body didn't really seem to be able to move – I felt sort of like my body had been numbed with Novocain to the point where I could feel and see them removing my bones but it didn't hurt. It reminded me of a time I had gotten stitches after a doctor had given me Novocain – it didn't hurt but I could feel them pull the thread through and tie each knot. My body was almost asleep in a way – it didn't really want to move. So I just watched as they removed my bones, then they seemed to count them and they started putting new bones back in after that.

I was totally confused – I had never heard of anything remotely like this, but I mostly just explained it away as a hallucination. After the new bones were back in they carried me back the way we had come and put me back in my room where my physical body was. The whole experience for some reason seemed very significant and important to me, but I couldn't have said why so I just moved on and didn't think that much about it.

But about 3 days later I was reading Supernatural, and the book described this same exact scenario down to the smallest detail calling this a "dismemberment". I had never heard of anything remotely similar to this before in my life, but suddenly it happens and then I read about the same experience only a few days later? What are the chances of that? And what are the chances of this happening multiple times with the same book and different visions I was having? I was experiencing synchronicities for the first time in my life and I didn't even know what a synchronicity was! And it wasn't just visions matching scenes from this book – I was having all kinds of weird coincidences that just didn't make sense... Events with seemingly perfect timing and deep meaning attached to them that seemed so impossible. I was wondering if either something terrific and magical was happening or maybe if I was going crazy! Had I stumbled into the spirit world or was I about to end up in a looney bin? I was certainly confused...

This book was describing my visions and the other people having similar visions. These other people having the same visionary experiences were Ayahuasca shamans from Peru and Brazil. I had never heard of Ayahuasca before and I hadn't really any clue what a shaman was, but here was someone experiencing what I was and they didn't call themselves crazy – they were healers and were part of an ancient tradition which used psychoactive plants as teachers and medicine. They connected to God and to the spirit world with psychedelic plants and in their communities they were not only accepted but they were respected. Their ability to explore this spirit world even led them to some otherworldly power to heal the sick and find answers to important questions their communities had. I wondered if these people might be able to help me understand what was happening to me. I also thought for the first time that maybe I wasn't crazy, and maybe everything I was discovering was real – after all, I wasn't the only one on this path and the path seemed to have real life benefits for me in a number of ways (most notably my mental and emotional health).

I also had some doubts reading this... After all, if these people could reliably heal others with these plants then why didn't the rest of the world know about this? I understood that maybe there were reasons for this information to be repressed like religious, political and financial reasons, but I was still skeptical. Part of me had this feeling that it was true, but I had a hard time really believing anything until I could experience it for myself. Something inside of me felt like I needed to make it down to South America somehow and attend a few ceremonies with these people. Part of that urge came from a curiosity to know the nature of reality and the spirit world, but there was also something else there that I couldn't explain – a feeling that this study and experience was somehow integral to my life in a way I couldn't understand until afterwards.

Challenges and Settling for Second Best

"I wonder if the snow loves the trees and fields, that it kisses them so gently? And then it covers them up snug, you know, with a white quilt; and perhaps it says "Go to sleep, darlings, till the summer comes again." ~ Lewis Carroll

I had a deep knowing that I wanted to travel to the Amazon to sit with real shamans, and I now heard that others were having authentic spiritual experiences too, but I was short on cash. I was in college part-time and working full time and I could barely afford to feed myself – there was no way I could afford traveling, and even if I did, how would I even find legitimate healers to sit in ceremony with? What if the healers I found lied to me or tricked me somehow? I decided to make the most of what I could find at home with the eventual goal of making it down to South America sometime in the future.

I didn't think anyone by me would be working with Ayahuasca but Supernatural had gotten me interested in shamanism so I decided to see if there was anything like a shaman where I lived. I didn't have much luck in my search. The only people I could find were some cheesy seeming new age people who taught "core-shamanism" and had no connection to traditional shamans in any way, but seemed to be playing more of a pretend game based loosely on shamanism. They also had ridiculously high prices that I couldn't afford and even if I could somehow scrounge the cash – I was hesitant to put my trust in these people without knowing if they were legitimate or not. It is one thing for someone to claim they are a shaman and a teacher, but I wanted to hear about real healings they had done. I had heard about fakes and phonies, and these people seemed to fit the bill.

So I kept learning as much as I could on my own. I got obsessed with reading – I started reading 1-2 books a week on spirituality and I attempted everything in the books that made sense to me to see what worked and what didn't. I invested a lot of my free time into this exploration. A lot of it was fun, and a lot of it was helpful in some ways... But looking back on it later I think a lot of it was less helpful then I had hoped. I think overall I ended up getting more from just following my heart and my intuition rather than books, but I guess I needed to get deep into the books for a while before I could see that there wasn't as much there as I had hoped. The entire process took me 4 years and over 100 books probably before I admitted to myself that the books weren't the best way to learn.

A lot of the authors I read tried to tell you their way was best – I guess they wanted to sell more books or something... It became really confusing with everyone telling me their way was best, because all of their ways were different! Some said to work with psychedelics, some said only meditate, some claimed I needed to learn advanced spiritual practices or fast or summon spirits or any number of things... Most just wanted me to visualize things and then believe they would come true from the "Law of Attraction" (this doesn't actually work – I tried!).

After reading many of these books and trying a bunch of the practices I found a specific area of interest and began to focus more there. Many of the books were telling me that meditation worked better then psychedelics and that psychedelics really interfered with your development... And while this didn't fit my experience I decided to give it a try. I decided to take a break from all psychoactive and mind-altering substances and focus solely on what I could do with my body and mind alone. Well, actually I then started getting all these different "magical" tools and learning all these practices and mantras ect – so a lot of this came from outside my body and mind still, but I decided to give this route a go and really commit to it.

I started practicing regular Buddhist meditation daily and also started doing other meditation with mantras daily. I didn't consider myself a Buddhist and disagreed with some parts of the philosophy, but I wanted to give the practice itself a fair try. At this time I also became very interested in tarot cards so I started working with them daily, and the tarot cards led me to being interested in Kabbalah and Gnosticism. Some people use Kabbalah and related practices to more deeply understand the tarot, and eventually I found there were many interesting books on Kabbalah, Gnosticism and on Western Occult. So I started researching and practicing some of these traditions alongside the mantras and meditations I was doing. I would generally spend 1-2 hours daily doing meditation and rituals this way, and sometimes I would spend a bit longer.

At first I was going into this on my own with just what I learned from books, but eventually I found two schools in my area that taught Kabbalah and Gnosticism and supposedly taught healing practices. I was a little skeptical, but at the same time very excited to have someone I could learn from. Deep down I really wanted to learn from shamans, but I didn't know any – and these people were right by home and offering to teach me! I thought it was the best thing ever at the time, and it wasn't till 3 years later that I finally wised up.

So this is how I ended up studying and practicing the traditions of a western occult "mystery school" and a Gnostic mystery school while also making my own studies and experiments with what I could find in books. Both of the schools I was with in hind-sight were more like cults then schools, but at the time I was really into the idea of being able to study and practice mysticism with others. Everything I was practicing seemed to fit well together as well – both of the schools mixed mystical practices from a number of different traditions into their teachings and I was basically doing the same with my own experiments so there wasn't too much contradiction. I stuck with this for 3 years straight – no mind altering substances and 1-2+ hours of ritual and meditation daily. I got really into this lifestyle and was fully committed to it, but afterwards I don't think it taught me as much or helped me as much as I thought it was during the time. In fact – I think overall it held me back and was more similar to brainwashing with meditation then about real mysticism.

Walking Meditations

"Above all, do not lose your desire to walk. Every day I walk myself into a state of well-being, and walk away from every illness. I have walked myself into my best thoughts, and I know of no thought so burdensome that one cannot walk away from it." ~ Soren Kierkegaard

Let's start simple and begin with what is close to home. Walking meditation is an easy practice that can sometimes be surprisingly powerful. The more remote in nature you are the more powerful the exercise becomes but it can even be done in a busy city – so anyone anywhere can do this meditation! During this practice we will focus on being more aware of our own bodies and the world around us – bringing intention and mindfulness to our walking. This style of meditation is often easier than sitting meditation for many people mostly because it is easier to be aware of your body and its sensations when you are moving and it can be difficult sometimes to focus on the subtle sensations of sitting meditation. We will learn a few different styles of walking meditation here.

This first method is to focus on self-awareness. It is good to practice this method first because the other methods are just slight tweaks or additions to this method. This can be done with shoes but if you are in nature it is especially fantastic when done barefoot!

Begin by simply standing. Feel the weight of your feet on the earth. Feel your body. Feel the breath in your body. Feel the subtle sensations of movement in your body as you balance yourself and stand – we take standing for granted sometimes but really this is a task complicated enough that it took you years to learn. Feel the slight movements as your body maintains its balance.

When you start walking do not change the way you walk – walk normal but just be more aware of your walking. A slow but normal pace is best – speed walking makes this harder.

Pay attention to your feet first. Feel the changes in sensation as your feet meet the ground and leave the ground. Feel the shift from heel, to ball of the feet to the toes. Feel the sensations all over your feet – not just where they touch the ground, but in-between the toes and how they feel in the air as you step. Feel the sensations of the earth on your bare feet or if you have shoes feel how your foot moves inside the shoe, how your shoes press against your feet and how the fabric of your socks feel. Pay attention to your ankles as well – how your joints feel as they balance on the ground or dangle in the air as you walk.

And try to let your body be relaxed while you do this. Slowly let your awareness rise from the ankles to the calves, knees, and thighs. Be aware of contact with your clothing and with the way your muscles are working together. Be aware of how your muscles feel.

Feel your belly and your chest. Feel your breath expand and contract within your body. Is your breath different now than when you were just standing? How are your shoulders moving? What do your arms feel like as they swing back and forth? Can you feel the air caress your arms as they move with each swing?

Next feel your neck. Feel the muscles supporting your head. If you relax the neck more does the position of your head change? Does your experience of walking feel different if you tuck your chin in more or if you hold it high in the air?

When you get to your head try to relax each part – your jaw and your eyes. Let the eyes relax and gaze gently ahead, without staring or being distracted to much with your surroundings.

You can be aware of the feelings that you're having; not in terms of emotions, but just the feeling tone. Are there things that feel pleasant or unpleasant – in your body, or outside of you? So if you notice things in your body that are pleasant or unpleasant, just notice them. Don't cling onto them, or push them away, but just notice them. If you notice things in the outside world that are either pleasant or unpleasant, just allow them to drift by – just noticing them without following them or averting your gaze from them.

This style of meditation can be done in any setting and be done anytime. It will help you learn and practice awareness which is a very valuable skill. It will also lead to relaxation and help you reduce stress and sometimes will provide useful insight about yourself and your life.

Mantras and Chakras

Mantras are used in many cultures and spiritual practices and can be a lot of fun. They can also help you focus during meditation and can help with cultivating awareness, cultivating compassion and developing other skills. Sometimes they are also a great way to raise or direct energy.

Usually you repeat a mantra many times to get a desired effect. You can time yourself and commit to 5-10 minutes of reciting the mantra, you can use a mala (prayer beads) to count your mantra, or you can just do the mantra as long as it feels right to you. You can also choose to chant, whisper, tone or sing the mantra which can all produce slightly different effects. If you do not know what toning is – it involves vibrating your voice through your whole throat and head as you push out air (think of someone "ohm-ing" and you will get the right idea).

Here are a few of my favorite mantras and what they are used for.

Om Mani Padme Hum – this is maybe the most popular mantra for many people to recite. It does not have a direct translation but is used to develop compassion and enlightenment.

Om Namah Shivaya – This is a very powerful mantra good for any situation including compassion and enlightenment. It is said to bring healing, love and peace. It also is good for protection.

Om Shree Dhanvantre Namaha– This mantra is calling on healing forces – either to create healing or teach healing.

Aham Brahma Asmi – Develop a sense of oneness with everything.

Aham Prema – I am divine love.

Ohm or **Aum** – Leads to liberation. Represents past, present and future as one.

Namu Myōhō Renge Kyō – reduce suffering by eradicating karma and also helping one attain a perfect awakening.

You can also do this practice with verses from holy scripture like the Bible, Bagavad Gita, Zohar or any other Holy book you enjoy. Other syllables that work well are the root syllables for the chakras.

The Chakras are an energy system that covers your entire body. It connects your subtle energy systems to the "physical" dense energy of your body. Often times these chakras may become imbalanced or blocked creating problems. Although there are hundreds of large and small chakras all over your body, there are commonly seven specific chakras along the spine that are paid more attention to.

Crown Chakra - Sahasrara: Soul purpose, link with God.

- Located at the pineal gland, or top of the skull (sometimes just above)

- Essence = Bliss, Toxicity = Attachment

- Tone of B above middle C

- Vowel sound is M

- Mantra is Aum

- Color is violet

Third Eye Chakra - Ajna: Imagination, clairvoyance, the balance between spiritual will and love.

- Essence = Vision, Toxicity = Illusion

- Located at the pituitary gland, or just above the eyebrow

- Tone of A above middle C

- Vowel sound is E

- Mantra is Sham

- Color is indigo

Throat Chakra - Vishuddha: Creative expression, clairaudience.

 - Essence = Truth/Communication, Toxicity = Lies or Withholding Communication

   - Located at the throat, particularly the vocal chords

   - Tone of G above middle C

   - Vowel sound is Eh

   - Mantra is Ham

   - Color is blue

Heart Chakra - Anahata: Balance between the souls love and will, healing ability, immune energies, love.

   - Essence = Compassion, Toxicity = Apathy

   - Located at the heart in the center of the chest

   - Tone of F above middle C

   - Vowel sound of Ah

   - Mantra is Yam

   - Color is green and pink

Solar Plexus Chakra - Manipura: Creative energy, hidden intelligence, intellectual mind, balance between feelings and thought.

   - Essence = Empowerment, Toxicity = Anger

   - Located at the navel

   - Tone of E above middle C

   - Vowel sound of O (as in God)

   - Mantra is Ram

- Color is Yellow

Sacral Chakra - Swadhisthana: Health, intuition, Kundalini energy.

- Essence = Peace, Toxicity = Shame/Guilt

- Located above the root chakra by the sexual organs

- Tone of D above middle C

- Vowel sound of O (as in oh)

- Mantra is Vam

- Color is orange

Root Chakra - Muladhara: Grounding of all spiritual energies, creation.

- Essence = Safety, Toxicity = Fear

- Located at the coccyx at the base of the spine

- Tone of middle C

- Vowel sound of long U

- Mantra is Lam

- Color is Red

To balance or open your own chakras, visualize them one at a time opening as spinning wheels. Start with the root chakra, and work your way up, visualizing with the appropriate colors. The root chakra faces down towards the Earth, the middle five chakras face front and back on your body, and the crown chakra faces up towards the heavens. To add to this balancing, or to balance the chakras of someone else, tone the appropriate mantra while visualizing and feeling the chakra open. If you can tone in the key of the chakra as well, this works even better.

There is much more to working with the chakras then this, but this is a good place to start. If you want to diagnose your chakras or someone else's the easiest method is to use a pendulum (you can buy or make a pendulum – either one should work). Hold the pendulum about two inches above yourself or your client as you lie down on your back. **If you are working on someone else, have them lay down as you stand or kneel over them and hold the pendulum over them.** If the chakra is balanced it should spin clockwise easily (might take a few seconds to start the pendulum spinning). If the spin goes counter-clockwise, goes up and down or side to side instead of a circle, or if it doesn't spin at all, then that chakra could use balancing. Best way to do this is start at the root chakra and work your way up – the first unbalanced chakra is the one you will work on. Afterwards you can test with the pendulum again to see how effective your work was.

Another way to diagnose which chakra you want to work on is to see how you or your clients issue matches up with the "toxicity" related to each chakra when it is out of balance. The crown when out of balance creates attachment (instead of bliss), 3rd eye creates illusion (instead of vision), throat creates lies (instead of truth), heart creates apathy (instead of compassion), solar plexus creates anger (instead of empowerment), sacral creates shame/guilt (instead of peace) and the root creates fear (instead of safety). By seeing which category someone's issue fits into you can find out which chakra might need to be balanced and you can test this with the pendulum.

One thing to note about this chakra system. This is one way of looking at the chakras and is not the only way. This is probably the most common and easy to use way. Some people work with only 5 chakras, or 8 chakras, or even 21 chakras ect... In traditional perspective the chakras are not things that exist objectively on their own, but are more of a system you can place in your mind to aid meditation and healing. If you read old tantric texts you will find they use chakras more as a place for directing energy – you often visualize words and symbols while toning sounds to focus energy into your body, or to move energy throughout your body. Over many years this 7 chakra system became very common and was used by many people, and the common understanding of the chakras changed. Now most people view them as objective energy centers that everyone has, but this is a newer view, not traditional. (Traditional does not always mean better though, and neither does newer – they are just different)

My understanding is that energy is formless and can take on any form that makes sense to you. If you understand this chakra system then when you decide to read energy that energy may choose to speak to you in the form of these chakras because that is an easy way for you to understand the energy. In reality the energy is formless and can appear in any way, but it appears in a way you understand so that you can communicate with and work with it. So don't worry too much about whether something is traditional or not – concern yourself more with whether or not it really works for you.

Losing Someone Special

Just before I had gotten into the mystery schools I was still in my phase of trying to learn on my own and really searching anywhere I could think of for answers and clues. I was working with a number of psychedelics as they seemed to be teaching me about this spiritual side of life... And they seemed to be healing my depression. In fact, after 3 years of working with psychedelics and just starting to get into meditation – my depression seemed to be gone.

I was realizing that where I used to be so dark and withdrawn, I was now experiencing more confidence and connection with others. I still got mad or sad sometimes when things were difficult – but it would last for a few minutes or maybe an hour or two instead of weeks or months at a time. It no longer overwhelmed me - something big had shifted. Life wasn't any easier – I was still broke and living on my own with my family spread across the country... But I wasn't depressed all the time anymore. I had passion, joy, excitement... And I loved myself and my life.

My mother wasn't doing so good though. She lived 5 hours away with my little sister and she was financially struggling and very depressed. Her doctor had her on all kinds of medications which didn't really seem to help and she struggled to find work. I know one of the hardest things for her was living so far away from my brother and me – the two of us and our little sister were all she really had. But she couldn't afford to move closer and I of course was broke and couldn't help her in any way that I knew of either.

But now I was starting to feel like I had healed at least the worst of my depression. I was learning a lot about meditation and Kabbalah. I wondered if I could share these things with my mother, but I didn't know how to bring it up. Most people are unfamiliar with Kabbalah and it can be a hard subject to explain for someone else when you are new to it like I was at the time. I also didn't know how she would react to me telling her about my psychedelic experiences. But I decided I needed to try and help her – so I wanted to invite her to try some psychedelics with me. Maybe it would give her hope to see this other side of reality – it had given me hope after all.

But I had taken too long… I was too depressed and scared to help her before, and now that I was ready – it was too late.

I remember I was taking an afternoon nap when my phone rang. It was a mysterious number and I somehow knew something was very wrong. I felt it – a feeling of trouble I couldn't explain. I answered the phone. My mother had committed suicide at the age of 45. I was 23, my brother was 21, and my little sister who lived with her was 16. She had overdosed on anti-depressants from her doctor which list as the first side-effect: "May increase chance of suicide." For some reason when she had told her doctor she was suicidal her doctor decided to prescribe something which studies show increases chance of suicide (sadly, this is common practice in Western medicine).

I thought I had cured my depression and this was the hardest test of that conviction that I could ever imagine. For 3 months I sunk back into my depression and I think it speaks to how much I had grown that it was only 3 months. After that depression it was still a year before my life started to feel normal without my mother, and I still miss her every day many years later… But I know things would have been much worse for me if I hadn't done that healing work before-hand. To tell you the truth – I probably would have followed my mother shortly after if I hadn't done that healing work.

Part of me felt lost… Part of me felt I had to be strong for my little brother and sister. Part of me felt like I had failed my mother by not helping her sooner… But my new state of mind wouldn't let me lie to myself that way. I knew taking the blame wasn't healthy for me, and so I tried to do my best to live a good life and honor my mother's memory.

I was still broke. My mother just killed herself. My girlfriend at the time had left for rehab and my best friend moved to another state. Before I got back from my mother's funeral many of my friends decided to start avoiding me without notice – I think they were scared I would be depressed when I got home from the funeral and they were too frightened to face me like that. I also got fired from my job and was struggling even more than normal. Somehow I survived though and for the most part even managed to stay positive.

The day after my mother died I wrote a song. I wrote the words and made a guitar riff I liked, but I couldn't bring myself to sing or play or practice it. The first time I played it was a few days later at her funeral – it was the first time my family had ever heard me sing. I was so sad about losing my mother, but at the same time I was glad to share my music with my family. It inspired me to think a bit more on creating beauty from suffering. That idea came to fruition a few months later at a festival.

I remember some friends and I wanted to make a large ritual out of a small festival. We talked about ritual theater a lot and about the ability of drama to inspire magic and healing within people. We found a spot in nature for the festival and started nature-scaping the whole place – using only what we could find in the forest around us we turned the whole area into a fairy wonderland setting. Arches made of branches, little tunnels and altars and art pieces made from stumps, stones and sticks... It was very beautiful and magical looking like some elven paradise from a storybook.

Since my friend and I designing the festival were both into Kabbalah we decided to insert symbolism of the tradition into the festival. We built a large fire to represent the center. The fire was the holy name of God – the Tetragrammaton which is 4 Hebrew letters which some pronounce as Yaweh or Jehovah. The name is written with 4 letters, but one is used twice so that 3 letters are used in the 4 letter name. YHVH. So there was a triangle around the fire to represent the first 3 letters YHV, and then the fire itself was the repeated H. Around the fire we placed 7 lampposts further out. These had the names and sigils of the Archangels carved into them as well as the next 7 Hebrew letters. Further out still were 12 stones with the Zodiac painted on them as well as the final 12 Hebrew letters. With the combination of the magical numbers 3, 7 and 12 we had used all 22 Hebrew letters and made the entire festival into a ritual.

We started the festival with a prayer and a performance combined as one "prayerformance". As my friend finished up this performance we invited everyone to crawl into a tunnel of arched branches – and at the end of the tunnel was a lady waiting with mushroom tea. People went into the tunnel one at a time and would offer a prayer as they were served a cup of mushroom tea to start the festival/ceremony.

After people drank their tea they would wander back to the fire where I was waiting with my guitar. I had designed 3 songs to go together as part of a musical ritual. Before playing I invoked spirits of music and healing and then I told people that I was offering a ritual they could participate in if they wished. I would play 3 songs – a song about calling forth the shadow, a song about letting go of the shadow, and another song about building something new in the empty space left by the liberated trauma. I told people they could offer something up that they wanted to release at this time – if they had an intention to let go of something and process it within these songs they could let the emotions of the song into them to work their magic.

The first song I sang was one I wrote after I found out my mother's death was a suicide. When she first died no one had told me the cause, and I didn't learn till 2 weeks later how she had actually died. People made it sound like a natural death instead of a suicide and I only learned the truth 2 weeks after the fact. That song called forth the anger, the pain – the shadow. Then I sang the song I had written for her funeral – a song about letting her go, and about her letting go of her body. The final song was "Wish You Were Here" by Pink Floyd and I asked the whole audience to sing along with me – this was creating community, art and beauty out of the pain. Sharing this experience took a vulnerability and openness I would have never had before, but allowed everyone in our group to connect on a deep heart-felt level.

I thought a lot about my mother, about music, about art and about ritual. Thought a lot about life and death and suicide. I wondered about God and about my path. I had started thinking before my mother's death that I wanted to be a healer of some kind... I wanted to help depressed people like myself and my mother – and now I felt that calling even more. I just didn't know how to answer the calling...

That was when I joined the mystery schools and started my 3 years of practice without entheogens. Of course it derailed me for a few years, but one very important lesson was learned from those schools: How not to act and what not to do in my practice.

Music Trance and Intention

"The earth has music for those who listen." ~ George Santayana

I spent a lot of time looking into different religions and spiritual practices, and while are all very unique, there are often some similarities. Three of the most common things I found through most traditions was a focus on sound, trance and intention. Religions speak about God creating with the word, or the original sound of creation and these things. And of course there are also many traditions which use medicine songs, worship songs, chanting and toning ect. Trance also plays a large role – often there are worship songs to put people into trance, drumming, dancing, meditation, fasting ect – the music and the trance state often have a interrelated relationship. Many different ways are used to enter the trance and the benefits of the trance can vary, but often there is some type of trance work. Intention might take the form of meditation or prayer – but it can also be as simple as wishing someone good will, or hoping to connect more deeply with the spiritual side of things.

I grew up playing music and since my early spiritual experiences were all produced by deep trance states I very quickly became interested in how to use music and trance to connect with spirit. There are many ways to do this, but some resonated more with me and that is where I really focused my time.

One example how to use magic in ceremony is the story I shared in the last chapter singing the 3 songs about calling forth the shadow, letting it go, and creating something new from that. This works on a few levels. The first level is the writing of the songs – this involves a therapeutic process of expressing your pain in a productive way to help you process it. You can do this with any art form – you could write a story or journal, you could paint or draw, you could even make jewelry or another craft that symbolizes the event or emotions being processed. Not only does it help you by providing a healthy outlet for processing trauma and pain, but it also gives you the chance to touch others with your art and help their process – which comes back to you again because now you also feel good for helping someone else!

Besides writing the songs there is also the experience of sharing them with others and performing them (this applies to other art forms as well). Expressing your pain to others in a healthy way can be extremely therapeutic. Figuring out how to accurately express things actually helps you understand things much better. Opening yourself up to vulnerability and sharing in that space is healing. So many aspects of this process are healing on many different levels.

And there is a third level of healing available here – using your intention. When I sang the 3 songs in the example here I told others that they could participate in the ceremony with me. So if people want to they can give themselves permission to be vulnerable and inspired, and the intention creates this space where inspiration and healing can occur. When you create this space and give yourself permission to be vulnerable and participate you can really open yourself up to miracles.

Intention can be very powerful even on its own. Let's say you have the intention to find medicine to help your healing path – in many ways it will seem as if you are then drawing medicines towards you, because your intention creates this space for you to pay better attention and seek things out, and helps you be more aware of the opportunities around you. There are so many things in our daily life which we don't notice because we aren't paying attention – there is too much information for us to process and acknowledge it all, so our brains filter out so much of the stimulus around us. But when you set an intention it really alters your filters and perceptions of the world around you.

When you take these basics of music or art and intention, and really explore how you can apply them in your life, the possibilities start to become endless. You may have heard of medicine songs before, and these songs can come in many forms. Some medicine songs are meant to inspire the emotions – heartwarming melodies or lyrics, or maybe even sad or emotional songs that you can relate to. By engaging the emotions through art you can skillfully inspire vulnerability and passion and so many other emotions that can help yourself or others find healing. Especially when coupled with meditation or plant medicines this engaging of the emotions can reach deep into past traumas or current emotions and stimulate deep healing.

Besides engaging the emotions you can also use music and art to move energy. This is what many shamans do with their medicine songs. In a plant medicine ceremony for example the shaman might see dark energy around the client and so they will sing to the plant spirits to help direct the healing of those dark energies. In a way the singer is then singing to the client and also singing to the spirits at the same time.

Using trance with intention and music provides even more possibilities. Trance can really help you get out of your head and focus more on your intuition. It can allow greater vulnerability and openness in many ways. Of course there are trances provided by plant medicines and psychedelics, but there are also trances created through meditation, sleep deprivation or sensory deprivation, fasting or dieting, breathwork, chanting, exercise or dancing, and also by music. Drumming can be a very fun and powerful way to enter and direct trance, and there are actually many shamanic cultures which focus on using tools like drumming, dance, or other music to enter trance instead of plant medicines.

Brainwashed – Mystery Schools and Cults

"Cherish those who seek the truth but beware of those who find it." ~ *Voltaire*

For a couple of years I fell into the same trap I still see many others fall into... I fell for the dogma and misdirection of groups making pleasant sounding but empty promises. These groups promised all kinds of things like deep knowledge of self, learning energy healing, mystical ascension and more, but never seemed to deliver on any of the promises. I would start to feel a little bit of energy so I thought it was working though – there was just enough there to make me think maybe the next class or next practice would do the trick... But each time was always empty and just pointed me towards buying another class or "healing". There were often small bits of truth and wisdom to be found, but those small bits of wisdom were surrounded by lies and dogma that was hard to separate from the truth.

One school was a path focusing on self-development only – lots of meditation and mantras and practice with lucid dreams. The practices were from all over the place – Rosecrucian and Theosophy, Buddhist, Hindu, Kabbalah ect... They called it gnostic, but it really had little to do with real traditional gnostic practices – mostly the philosophy behind the practices was gnostic and they believed in the demi-urge (the demi-urge is a gnostic idea that the Old Testament God was actually an evil tyrant called the demi-urge and that there is another higher God above it). The main issue with this school was that the practices were only somewhat effective and required a lot of time, and they came along with a lot of dogma from the schools founder who was a racist, sexist, and homophobic guru. I remember sitting in class and thinking that the teachers were sweet and nice, the practices were nice, but then I would read the writings of the schools guru founder and would just see hate and ignorance masquerading as spiritual enlightenment. I wanted to learn so badly that for a while I overlooked the parts of the school I didn't like.

The other school was much worse. They claimed to be focused on self-development and healing but their main focus was business and the whole school was a giant pyramid scheme. Everything in the school came from one leader who claimed to be a Golden Dawn initiate, and all the rituals were rip offs from the Golden Dawn, but more watered down and even less effective. At the time I was really into the Golden Dawn, so I thought this was great to be learning similar practices, but if you ever look into Golden Dawn for yourself you will find that the system isn't very effective for anyone practicing it (it took me a couple years to admit the Golden Dawn was an incomplete path). It makes giant claims about how you will master yourself and the world around you, yet many of the Golden Dawns highest initiates actually died as frauds, or were poor, alone, addicted to drugs or haunted by endless lawsuits.... So you can see that the system mostly just inflates people's egos! The funny thing is, after leaving this school I read papers written by Golden Dawn initiates like Dion Fortune and Waite where they described their experience with the Golden Dawn the same way I was experiencing this modern school – that there were lots of empty promises and just enough energy to keep you coming back, but you never really get what you hoped for.

This "mystery school" makes a lot of promises, but they never deliver. They give you just enough that you come back for more, but really it is a vacuum of resources and money and time that leads you astray from your true potential. They sell healing after healing, but the healings dont actually help any illnesses - they are more like pretend healings. If you tell them you are sick, they tell you to go to the doctor and then tell you about their healings and how you need them all. Right after you get a healing, they tell you that you promptly need another healing and also a class. If you ask them what these healing heal, you will get dodgy answers with lots of New Age mumbo jumbo that doesn't really tell you anything (they will claim something heals your DNA or connects you to your divine blueprint or something else silly, but can't tell you what the effects or benefits of it are in real down to earth terms). They also claim that just about every famous person who has ever lived is a part of their school no matter when they lived or what religion they belonged to – with no evidence to back this up, and lots of evidence out there to contradict it. It is kind of a weird system, and looking back I really wonder how I ever fell for it. I think really that I just wanted to learn so badly and I wanted to share my studies and work with other like-minded individuals – so I often ignored what I didn't like so I could be a part of this community that seemed to offer the things that I wanted.

A lot of people in cults like this are smart and nice people. You like them and become friends and in some ways you assume they know more because they have been in the school longer... You wonder if maybe there is a phase in the school where things suddenly make sense and you understand it all. But it never comes. When other people tell you the school is stupid you get defensive because you want to defend your friends who are all nice and well-meaning, but who inadvertently mislead people. This all pulls you further into the cycle. You really want to believe the stories they tell you and you invest so much time and money... It becomes very hard to admit you were wrong all along. It becomes a vicious cycle that is hard to find your way out of, and I totally fell for it.

So I got deep into this school. I practiced all their rituals daily or even twice a day. I worked for some of the oldest and most high up students and teachers of the school. I got to see behind the scenes and learned more than most about this school. I spent thousands of dollars on their classes and healings and traveled to other countries sometimes for international programs.... I am embarrassed to say I even promoted this school and sold some of the fake healings myself. I really believed in them at the time, though there was a skeptical part of me that I always had to repress. I believed in what I was telling people, but sadly I had fooled myself before perpetuating the cycle on others. I gained a false sense of community, but in the process I was starting to lose myself.

I've always been a skeptical person. But I had gotten swept up in this new side of reality – the spiritual side of things, and while I knew this spiritual world was very real, I didn't know much about it. I wanted to learn everything. Part of me thought that to really get into it I just had to trust and try everything, and then maybe test things out later to see what really worked and what didn't.... If you are skeptical about something in the process and keep questioning each move you make it is often hard to really give something a fair chance and fully commit to the process. But I let it go on for too long and it got out of hand. Luckily the skeptical voice I had started to repress never gave up – I always came back to a few questions, and these questions eventually pulled me back to reality.

I know some people out there think nothing spiritual should cost money, and I get where they are coming from…. But I don't necessarily agree. I do think that it should be attainable to all who need it though, and this does require some moderation to any costs, and fair costs that even the sick can afford. At a certain point costs do become ridiculously high and unethical – so there really needs to be a balance. In the "mystery school" a class may cost $1,000 for 2 days after which you went home the same as before. Half of the class often seemed to be a sales pitch for other classes and healings. Obviously most people cannot afford things like this, and the prices seemed out of balance to me for the amount of time and work put in by those offering the healings and classes. I worked for one teacher who could make $20,000 in a single weekend off of her students, and while that is great for her, I also know that many of those students were going deep into debt for this, or missing classes because they couldn't afford them. For some this even led to people losing jobs, losing houses, or fighting within their family – in some cases even divorce that left children in broken homes. I saw firsthand what the demands of this school could do to people's lives and it was not pretty. If you couldn't afford the next class in some cases they would say you don't deserve to be in the school anymore and would kick you out!

The "mystery school" always said if you did the rituals then the energy would be there for you and the money would follow that. For 3 years I did every ritual they showed me 1-2 times a day (they recommended once a day but I was an overachiever). Most people never practiced the rituals outside of class. In class I would often know as much about subjects as the teachers and I was obviously studying everything they gave me and then some…. Other students would just show up to class once a month and that was the only effort they put in, no daily rituals or outside study. But I didn't make much money and had trouble moving forward in the classes since I couldn't afford them. Other people who had money but didn't care about the practices moved forward ahead of me all the time. I started wondering why the school seemed to benefit wealth more than skill, practice, or dedication to the tradition. I wondered what spiritual system rewards money more than effort and dedication?

I also saw how much many of the students lied and repressed their true selves in order to be better salespeople for the school. I mentioned I worked for a teacher who could make tens of thousands in a single weekend and she was always busy making money.... Yet she was totally broke. She made so much cash, but she spent it all on the school – because the further you go into the school the pricier it gets. Each class costs more than the last and the teachers had to keep taking the most expensive classes of all. This teacher claimed to be the master of her life and of herself... But she was just as broke as all the people who couldn't afford her classes. For this story we will call her Annette (real name changed for privacy). She was deep in debt and just putting on a show. And she wasn't the only one – it seemed like almost all of them were this way.

I remember talking to another woman in the school about her personal dreams. She had this dream to be a clothing artist – and she made awesome clothes that totally could have supported her if she put in the time. But she said she had to focus on selling "mystery school" classes instead because the teachers told her it was more important... She gave up her dream to sell someone else's dream, and I always wondered how this could be in her highest good? She was so deep into the school but so distraught, and she went around telling people she had found the one true way to enlightenment with this school... Never admitting that it wasn't even the right way for her, much less anyone else.

And there was also an issue very close to my heart. The school claimed any mind altering substances were bad, and that cannabis was horrible for anyone on a spiritual path and so were all other plant medicines. This was very confusing for me because my experience really told me otherwise. Psychedelics had opened up the spiritual world to me and started me on this path after all. My work with this school was during my 3 year break from all mind altering substances though, so I was deeply committed to their system... I just kept wondering about these plant medicines, because something told me I was missing out by neglecting them.

One of my best friends in the school was also a teacher in the school. We will call him Steve. He was one of the higher up students and had gone deeper in the school than most. He always tried to make it seem like he supported himself by doing classes and healings, but truth was he grew cannabis. Almost all of his income was from his cannabis grow and he only made little bits of cash here and there from the school classes he taught – just not enough people were interested in the high prices. But he would always preach about how bad cannabis was and about how the school would lead to abundance and success…. And funny enough – the school unknowingly held some of their most important rituals above his grow room without knowing it.

One day another friend of mine smoked cannabis before attending the important "ritual temple" they did every week. We will call this friend Wilson. Annett had learned before the ritual started that Wilson had smoked a little bit, and so she planned a mean game to make an example out of him. After the ritual she claimed that the spirits were pissed and had told her that he had smoked cannabis and that he had ruined the temple with his "negative energy." Even though he had spent thousands of dollars on the school they kicked him out to make an example because too many of the students were smoking cannabis against the schools wishes and they wanted to control everyone. He was heartbroken and really believed the story that spirits had told her this. Until I told him that she had known beforehand and another student had tattled on him. Weird how she would have to make up this game to play with him right? Honesty seems like a better route to me, but this was "the mystery school" after all.

Funny thing was – their temple had been above a grow room for a few years straight and that had never caused any issue that she noticed. She was totally unaware of the grow room under her temple, or that one of the temple participants watered and fed and sold cannabis plants on a daily basis.

So I had all these questions…. Why so judgmental and ignorant about plants and psychedelics? Why were so many people in the school depressed, dishonest, and broke or in debt? Why would people progress if they didn't do any rituals or practice but had money, but those doing all the work wouldn't progress? Why didn't any of the healings really heal anything? Why were there so many holes in the story?

Well, around this time I had started dating someone very special. I introduced her to the "mystery school" and she did a few classes with me and we were both living without mind altering substances... But one weekend we were camping and I decided to test out the effects of doing ritual with psilocybin mushrooms. It had been 3 years since I had done anything like this and I wanted to see if the sober meditation focus was really better for me then working with the plant medicines.

I could remember the deepest experience I had ever had with the "mystery school." At the end of a 10 month class we had a 3 day retreat where we were meditating and doing ritual about 10 hours a day for 3 days. At the end of 3 days we took a break fro their curriculum and I went out by myself to pray alone under a tree... I felt the sky open up and a presence talk to me. I felt God speak to me the way I had felt it the first time I tried mushrooms years before. Funny how it had taken me a 10 month class and a 3 day retreat and thousands of dollars to get me where one nibble of mushrooms had years before.... And this happened when I was just by myself outside, not when I was in the class following their structure.

So I was thinking of that day from class when my girlfriend and I decided to eat mushrooms. We ate the mushrooms outdoors in nature and went for a hike. Trees started talking to me. Clouds took on shapes of angels and animals. At once point the sky and the earth both opened up – and I felt a moment of talking to Mother Earth and to God at the same time... I learned more about myself and God in this one day then I had in the previous 3 years meditating or attending the mystery schools. I knew meditating had helped my development, but I also knew that plant medicines were the path for me. By this time I had read a little more on shamanism and I decided I wouldn't work with the chemical psychedelics, but just with the ones provided by God in nature. I would leave these mystery schools and try to find my own way.

And that is when I felt the forests start calling me. The plants started calling me again. And Peru called me once more. I felt this calling in my heart and decided to just go for what I really had wanted all along. No more excuses and no more settling.

Introduction to Core Shamanism

When I finally left the two mystery school cults I had been working with I was so glad to be out and knew it was the only right choice…. But I also felt this confusion and a little emptiness. The schools and their philosophy had become such a large part of my life that when I left I really struggled to process my beliefs and views. Where did my beliefs come from? From my life and personal experience, or from the school? I had built so much of my identity around these groups and my involvement with them that in some ways I felt like I suddenly didn't know myself and this was very hard.

One example of this was that every morning when I was in these cults I would spend 30-60 minutes doing ritual and meditation. But these were mainly rituals and meditations that I learned from these groups and they didn't really feel right to me anymore. I didn't believe in them. But one benefit they had given me when I was performing them daily is a sense of comfort and routine. They helped me focus, center and ground myself, and they also gave me a place to process some emotions. But they couldn't help me in that way anymore – because now all I could think about was how fake and phony they were and how much time I was wasting each day with these repetitive practices. I knew that I needed to replace these practices with something else because I saw the benefits of having some sort of spiritual practice in my life, but I wanted one more real and authentic.

For the first month I didn't really do any meditations or ritual. After a while though I was thinking about what really called me the most and I realized that my true passion and interest had always been shamanism, and that I had just gone down this western occult path because it was more readily available to me. So I decided I should just focus on shamanism and stop settling. I would look for a good teacher, but if I couldn't find any – I would just learn on my own. At least with learning on my own I wouldn't have to settle for poor teachers or someone teaching me their dogma.

At this time I was about two years into a relationship with the women who later became my wife. Her name is Tasha and from the start of our relationship we had always been very close and near inseparable. I just mentioned in the last chapter how we decided to test out magic mushrooms again, as it had been 3 years for me since I had worked with any psychedelics. We went camping in the mountains and ate some mushrooms at the start of a small hike. I remember the forest came to life and the trees were talking to us. At one point I looked up into the sky and I could swear that the sky opened up and I talked to God for a moment that felt like eternity. I learned more about myself and God in that one afternoon then I had in the previous 3 years meditating and doing ritual. I didn't know if plant medicines were going to be my path or not, but I knew I had at least a little more exploring in this area still.

So Tasha and I knew at this point that we wanted to keep teaching ourselves for a bit. I was looking into some books for inspiration and a few books on core shamanism found their way to me. I was a little unsure about core shamanism as I really wanted to learn something more traditional, but I thought I would at least give it a chance and see where things went. I have to admit – I was attracted by the idea that there was a common thread through shamanic practice that people could focus on learning without appropriating other cultures.

If you are unfamiliar with core shamanism, basically it is a western style of neo-shamanism which looks at the more superficial levels of shamanic practice and tries to create a generic practice based on the similarities from other shamanic cultures. It most heavily focuses on "shamanic journey" work which is a style of meditation where you send your consciousness out of your body to look for guidance and healing. This is usually a very visual type of meditation and while some people do it just with meditation, many people use practices to help them enter a trance when they do this – such as breathwork, or most commonly drumming. We started testing this tradition out by focusing on the drumming and rattling.

The basic philosophy behind the core shamanism model is similar to many shamanic philosophies. There is a lower world, a middle world and an upper world all connected through the "world tree." When you do shamanic journey you can visit these 3 worlds and each has a different purpose or resource. The middle world is our world. This is where we live. The upper world is a heavenly type realm where you go to seek teachers and guidance – especially about spiritual matters. The lower world is a place to seek healing and power and in the core shamanic perspective this is mostly where you work with power animals (you still often work with power animals in all 3 worlds, but especially in the lower world).

When you first start learning core shamanism it is usually recommended that you journey to the lower world first and seek your power animal there. In some traditions they say you have one power animal and in some traditions they say you have many. One thing you learn quickly about core shamanism – everyone experiences it different and there aren't a ton of rules. You learn the generic style first, but after that you are encouraged to develop your own style. So the idea here is that you may start with a little opening ritual or intention setting, but the journey itself is done with drumming. Often times they tell you to do your first journey or two, and then once you have connected with a power animal or guide – have them teach you your opening ritual, so sometimes your first few journeys have less opening ritual.

A lot of the classes on core shamanism don't go as deep as I would have liked, but they did give us a good foundation to build our own practices from. Tasha and I practiced journey work almost every day and for a while we really learned a lot from it. Mostly it helped us get in better touch with our own hearts. When we made our own ceremonies with plant medicines we would even factor in some of the ideas from core shamanism and let our intuition guide us the rest of the way – and this especially helped us a lot. We especially found this style of journey work to be helpful before and after plant medicine ceremonies to help us get more clarity around what we learned from the plants. When we had problems we couldn't figure out or when we felt stuck in an emotional pattern that wasn't serving us we would do some journey work to help us navigate to solutions. It was especially helpful for us in our relationship together and helped us find many insightful ways to appreciate each other and bond more deeply.

Shamanic Journey

There are many ways to perform and practice shamanic journey. I will explain the basic ideas and most common way it is taught first, and then I will suggest some alternative options that you can explore if you like. I will also describe how to do this practice without any opening ritual first – and we will talk about possible opening rituals afterwards. One thing I do like to mention – this is based mostly on core-shamanism which is not a traditional shamanic practice, so there really isn't a right or wrong way to do this – what is most important is how well it works and whether or not it benefits you and others.

As with most meditation practices you want to begin by making sure you are somewhere you can comfortably try this meditation without distractions. You want to silence your phone and not be busy with anything else. You can be outdoors or inside. A dim room or dim lighting can be helpful but isn't required. You will also need a few things for this practice: a blindfold of some kind and also a percussion sound. The percussion sound can either be a frame drum or a rattle, but most people find it easier with the drum. If you are trying this on your own, it can be hard to journey and drum at the same time, so many people like to use a recording of a drum made specifically for this meditation. You can find "shamanic drumming" or "journey music" online or even on YouTube.

If you use a recording of drumming music you can play it on speakers, but most prefer to use headphones. It should be fast repetitive drumming and it is best if it plays for 10+ minutes so that you don't get cut short in your meditation. If you are using a live drum or rattle it is best if you have a partner who can drum for you – you can find videos on YouTube to get the right drumming speed down. You can drum on your own for yourself, but this is a lot harder to learn and may distract you from your journey unless you practice enough to get proficient.

Whenever you have everything set up for your meditation you can take a second to get yourself into a meditative and receptive state of mind. This can be done with opening ritual or it can be done with some deep breathing and relaxing. When you feel receptive you can start the drumming track or have your partner start drumming for you. You can sit up but most people find it easier to journey while lying down. If the room isn't very dark you will either want a blindfold over your eyes or if you don't have one, some people journey with an arm over their eyes to create darkness. Make sure you are comfortable so you can focus on your journey without distractions. Take a moment to focus on your intention for your journey – if this is your first journey I suggest your intention to just be traveling your tunnel to the lower world and then returning. The lower world is one of 3 worlds that you can journey to (the lower, middle and upper worlds) and is usually the best place to start. We will discuss the 3 worlds more in depth soon.

As you lie down and listen to the drum take a moment to let the drumming wash over you. Feel your body vibrate with the drum. Let your mind relax and let everything but the drum drift out of your awareness. As you feel yourself deepen into a light trance state start to visualize a place in nature that you know which has some type of hole into the earth. This can be a cave, a burrow, a hollowed out tree stump, or any other hole into the earth that feels appropriate to you. You should choose a location and a hole that feels safe and inviting and I recommend picking one spot and sticking to it as you continue this practice.

As you visualize the hole that you chose, look around the environment the hole is in and notice the details of where you are. Turn until you are facing the hole and take your time really seeing and experiencing your vision of that hole. Move towards it and go inside. Inside you will be in a tunnel. Take your time to really see what the tunnel is like. Feel the walls. Feel the earth under your feet. Notice if the tunnel is dry or damp and let yourself breathe in all the details. Let yourself move through the tunnel at whatever speed feels right to you. You can fly or walk – whatever you find yourself doing naturally, just go with that.

The tunnel may wind or turn – keep following it. If you run into any obstacles don't worry about them – just go around them and continue into the tunnel. If you get stuck somehow, go back, and start over. Eventually you should come to the end of the tunnel – let yourself exit the tunnel into the lower world.

The lower world may look like anything. Don't judge it – just experience it for a moment and let it be what it is. Often times the lower world looks like some sort of nature scene – maybe a garden, a lake or a beach, maybe forest, or anything else. After taking a moment to look around go back into your tunnel and go back the way you came all the way to where you started, and back to your physical body. When you feel like you are back to your physical body you can take your time opening your eyes and sitting up. If you like, write down anything you experienced that you want to remember later.

For your first journey I don't recommend staying in the lower world for very long. Just go in and experience it for a little, and then return. There is at least one more journey you should do before exploring very far – you should journey to meet your first power animal.

To journey and meet your power animal you will do what you did for the first journey, but take a second before starting to focus on your intention – to journey to the lower world and receive your power animal. This time, as you exit your tunnel into the lower world start exploring and look for your power animal. You know you have found your power animal when you see the same animal 4 times – so if you see multiple animals, wait till one of them enters your vision 4 times. You may see the whole animal each time, or you may see just parts of the animal – seeing a part of the animal still counts as seeing the animal. So you might see a deer eye, then a whole dear, then just the antlers, and then the whole deer again – that is 4 times so you know that is the animal you are supposed to bring back. Give the animal a hug and hold it tight (you can hug it in your vision while at the same time physically hugging with your body). Try to keep the animal in this embrace so you can bring it back with you – with the animal still in a hug go back into your tunnel and back to your physical body. When you get back to your physical body take a second to feel the animal you are hugging enter your body and merge with you. When you are ready you can slowly open your eyes and sit up. You now have your power animal with you and can ask them to teach you and guide you and protect you on your future journeys! (If you like, take a second to write down anything interesting from your journey)

While we are discussing the journey for power animals, I will also mention that the method for connecting someone else with their power animal is the same as the method for finding your own. Just start with the intention to find the animal for the person you are journeying for. If you have them there in person you can perform the journey lying down next to them, and if they aren't there, take a second to connect energetically with them in your mind, and imagine them lying next to you while you journey. When you hug the power animal and bring it back to your body, sit up while still hugging the power animal, and then use your breath to blow the power animal into their heart 3 times and into their crown 3 times. If they are not in the room with you then just imagine them in front of you while you blow and take a second to really visualize them with the power animal.

Your power animal is helpful for many things. Since you are learning how to journey the power animal is especially helpful to you – it can act as your guide and protector and companion on your journeys. The power animal can also become your teacher and once you have a strong connection with your power animal, as long as you are willing to put in the time and work, your power animal can teach you all about how to journey deeper and how to heal. Retrieving a power animal for someone else is a very easy way to help connect others with their power. Even if they aren't consciously connecting with the power animal afterwards, the connection you helped create during the journey experience will still produce benefits in their life such as good luck, better protection, more confidence ect…

In some traditions a person only has one power animal, and in other traditions a person can have many. I would trust your intuition about yourself and try to develop experience with your journey work so that you can trust your journeys as well. When you learn about something in your journey try to integrate it into your life to get the most benefits from it. When you journey for someone else, always make sure you ask what they experienced during your journey, and try to follow up with them to see if they had any lasting benefits afterwards – you may be surprised how much this work can benefit some people.

3 Worlds

In many shamanic and animistic cultures people consider reality to be made up of 3 worlds: the lower world, middle world and upper world. The associations and descriptions of the 3 worlds sometimes differ slightly from culture to culture, though the 3 worlds always seem present. The lower world is a place of power and in the core shamanic tradition is where you discover your power animals. You often journey here to find and create power. The middle world is our regular reality we live in day to day. Often times many people don't journey here as much, and that can be a shame. There is a lot to do in middle world journeys – visit places around the world, test your skills, certain types of healing work can be done here, and you can also journey into places or people that you want to help to see if any illness or heavy energy makes itself known to you. The upper world is a heavenly type realm where you often go for guidance. Some of the best teachers live in the upper world so there are a lot of reasons to go here when you need clarity or insight.

In this style of journey work that we are looking at right now, most people will follow the route of first journeying to the lower world to connect with their power animal. Once that is done you have many options of where to journey and what to journey for next. Some people may want to do a few more journeys with their power animal in the lower world to get to know their power animal better – maybe you even want to ask them for some guidance and healing with an issue you have. What is most important at this stage is getting lots of practice – you need experience and practice to get good at this technique and to be able to test and trust your results. The practice is easy to have small successes with right away – such as meeting your power animal, but it takes a lot of time to develop this skill to where you can get deeper results with healing work and more specific guidance. As your experience grows and your relationships with your spirit guides grow stronger – you will be able to accomplish more.

There are a few other journeys which can be very helpful to do at this point. One of these is to first journey to the lower world and check in with your power animal, and then to ask them to help you reach the upper world and to introduce you to your first upper world guide. There are many ways to get to the upper world, and once your power animal shows you how to get there, you can go straight to that path instead of having to visit the lower world first and then go up. Many paths seem to be common for upper world journeys. Some people climb a rope into the sky, some may climb a tree into the sky, other people might climb a mountain into the sky or just fly straight up.... Usually as you enter the upper world there is a feeling or sense of crossing a sort of veil – like passing through a soft barrier. Once you have passed this veil you are in the upper world.

When you meet new spirit guides there are a few methods to check and make sure it is really your guide and teacher. In the case of this journey with your power animal to the upper world your power animal can vouch for the spirit you meet and introduce you. Often one of the better ways to check if a spirit is your teacher is to ask your other guides. You can also check with the spirit by asking "Are you my teacher here for my highest good?" Your real guide should give you a straightforward answer to this question. For this specific meditation and for meeting your main upper world guide there is also one more test you can give – ask them to bring down the sun. If they can make the sun rise and set in your upper world visions this is a good indicator they have a special relationship with you. Once you have confirmed these two guides (your main power animal and main upper world guide) then you can ask them for confirmation when you meet other spirits you don't know.

A power animal is always some type of animal. Your upper world guide however can take on many forms. It can be a person, an old "god" such as Greek or Egyptian gods, a transforming spirit or part animal and part human spirit, or maybe it looks more spirit like and less like a person – it really could take on many forms, but generally there are some human like features at the least. While the power animal helps you more with healing work and finding lost power, the upper world guide is more of a teacher and guide for your spirit and life. Often times you can go to the upper world for guidance and insight and learning, and go to the lower world for more healing purposes. Sometimes you may go to the lower world for learning or the upper world for healing as well, so these are more generalities then hard and fast rules – trust your intuition on where to journey to, and if you go to the wrong spot first your guides there will point you in the right direction quickly.

The middle world is the world we live in. It has this physical side we all know so well, but also a very strong energetic side. Often times you will journey here to either find things, or to help with healing. This is also a good place to journey to when testing the accuracy of your journeys – for example, you can journey to a store you have never visited and see the basic layout of the store, then walk there in person later and see how accurate you were. You could also journey into someone's body or chakras for example and find causes of illness or energy that needs rebalancing too.

In different traditions the 3 worlds may have more specific layouts or characteristics. For now we will work with this model, but we will cover the 3 worlds from more perspectives throughout this book.

Dancing Your Animals And Hallow Bone

"When we become hallow bones there is no limit to what the higher powers can do in and through us in spiritual things." ~ Frank Fools Crow

Before continuing on to our story I want to cover one more topic of working with spirit guides and power animals. When you develop the relationship with your guides far enough you can learn to channel those spirits through you. There are many ways to do this and many purposes can be achieved with this practice. One concern though is you only want to do this with spirits you really trust and who you know have your best interests at heart – don't just let any spirit work through you, or you may find yourself in trouble.

The first method I learned of working in this way has to do with connecting with and expressing your power animals. You can open your ceremony or sacred space with any ritual you feel called to include and do any preparation work you like to get you in the mood. When you are ready begin with the intention to let one of your power animals dance through you – any power animal of yours that wants to dance. Start drumming or rattling or making music to help you enter a trance, and start swaying, moving, and dancing a little bit. Try to let your inspiration and feelings guide you, and don't think about what you are doing too much. Try as much as possible to go into a trance while doing this and try to let your power animal really express yourself.

You may start to feel like you are an animal, or see yourself as an animal. You may feel like you are flapping your wings or swinging your tail. You may start making sounds – maybe animal sounds or something else – just let it flow out. Let yourself go. Really let yourself feel the power animal dancing through you.

Dance like this for as long as you feel called to – you can end at any time. The practice feels stronger the more you do it and the more open you become. This is a good way to connect more with your power animals and it also gives them a chance to experience physical reality through you – almost like a way to sort of feed them a bit. It can also help develop your intuition and helps you get ready for deeper practices along these lines. This is also a great warm up for deeper journey work – it helps you connect with your spirit guides and get into a deeper trance before starting the journey.

Sometimes I like to do deeper merging with spirit guides. When I do this I personally like to sing a song or two to get me in the mood, raise my energy, and also start connecting with the spirits. I think you could easily insert passionate prayer or a conjuration for this instead of singing or dance your animal first. Then I either drum, or rattle, or just dance and sing myself into a frenzy. You could do it without this percussion, but I use the percussion to help me enter a trance (often I have a partner drum for me while I rattle). I also use the rattles quite often during the trance for breaking up energy or doing other energy work, so they double as a magical tool and trance aid. I will usually chant/sing and sway while rattling to enter a good trance - holding the intention now, that I am merging with my power animal.

Eventually, the spirit is connected to you deeply enough to work through you. Your arms may look like the spirits arms (or claws or wings ect in case of power animals), and you may make strange sounds or speak words you don't know (I make animal sounds sometimes, or sing a song I've never heard before). Do whatever work you came to do, and then afterwards tell the spirit you are done, and let them fade away as you calm down from the trance and also ground yourself in some way (wiggle around, feel your body again, eat ect). Using this method you may work on clients or do deep healing work by letting the spirit work through you and create healing.

Types of work you can do with this method:

-See illness or misplaced energy in someone's body

-See astral/spirit world around you through your eyes

-Perform Extraction type work or even exorcisms

-Learn to use new magical tools

-Communicate with the spirit, or with other nearby spirits

-Protection

For protection, while you are merged with the spirit, it protects you. This is why I sometimes do extraction work this way - the energy I am pulling out doesn't ever touch me, because the spirit is the one doing the work. It provides a powerful shield. Also, the spirit usually knows what to do better than I do, as extraction is their specialty, so it also allows their expertise to be used fully. One teacher told me you know when you are fully merged, because there is no fear in you any longer - if you have any fear, it means you need to keep merging/connecting with the spirit and enter a deeper trance. Once you are fully merged, you are filled with the power of that spirit (power-full), and protected.

Because you may not know what spirits to use for what work, it is often a good idea to journey and ask your spirit guides what work they specialize in, or to ask for a volunteer from your guides to help you do extraction work or whatever other work you may be doing.

For using a magical tool, I will ask a spirit to merge with me to teach me about the tool. This allows any spirit with expertise with that tool to volunteer. I will go through the same process of merging with the spirit, then once merged, they will pick up the tool and just start using it. This is how I learned to use a number of my magical tools.

You could get really creative with this - there are all kinds of possibilities!

Sometimes this type of work is called "hallow bone" healing, because in a sense you are not doing any healing work – you are being a hollow bone to channel energy from your spirit guide, and it is the spirits working through you creating the healing with the clients participation. If you master this technique there is really no limit to the work you can learn to do, and most energy healers and shamans I have met use some version of channeling their spirit guides through themselves.

I had one particularly interesting experience with a client. We had an extended time to work together in person, and this was exciting for me, as most clients can only spend a few hours with me, a day at most, or just want help online. But since I had so much time with the client, I was really able to let go and trust the spirits.

This client had a number of deep rooted issues they wanted to work on, so I decided to call in my two most rusted allies: San Pedro and Redwood Tree. I knew by calling on these two spirits, I could just sit back, and watch the clients journey with spirit unfold. So, we brewed our medicine, and took a road trip to the Coastal Redwood forests. Each morning, we would sing a song in ceremony, call in sacred space, give offerings of tobacco, set an intention, perhaps drink some medicine, and start a hike through epic redwood forest.

When you let the spirits work through you, everything falls into place and especially in a setting like the redwoods or any other epic nature locale - Spirit will speak to you through the world around you. Including a powerful medicine teacher like San Pedro makes this even more life changing and powerful!

When you are receptive you can find all kinds of ways to embrace the medicine around you and become connected to the flow of the medicine. In this particular experience we were hiking, and came across a giant over-turned and hallowed out log. We could walk past it, but it caught my eye, and I told the client "Here you must climb through, so you can be reborn on the other side!" I let the forest inspire this idea within me and then suggested the perspective to the client - they listened, and the tunnel-log became a sort of initiation. This particular log was very long and skinny, and pretty scary to climb through - but we must learn to overcome fears, and the forest provided this opportunity. As this friend climbs through the tree he gets really scared and wants to turn around but I urged him on – suddenly as he is in the middle of this 30 foot hollow log – he sits down and says "I am not scared anymore!" He wasn't only not scared of the tree anymore, but suddenly had personal insights about his life and faced emotions he was previously scared of – his training with the tree turned into personal realization and insight about his life. When they need someone to talk to, I just listen attentively and support them, but don't teach them or guide them - the medicine will show them what they need to see, and they only need you to remember they are supported.

Next on our Redwood hike, an urge to grab the rattle arises. A song from Spirit springs forth from my lips (a song I had never heard before), and since I am just following Spirit, I let it fill the forest. I don't know the words of the song, and just trust them to come - incidentally, my voice does things I don't know how to make it do, and makes words I don't know normally, but I understand in the moment anyways. Suddenly - the client's energy and mood has shifted after visions brought on by the song (in this particular experience the client said the song turned into a vortex that took them on an inner journey).

While exploring the forest perhaps an animal or bird comes along with a lesson, or perhaps a shiny rock makes itself noticed from the ground - a new ally and piece of medicine to take home. Perhaps a certain river or tree stands out to you - so here we would place another offering of tobacco, or take a break to meditate. Everything comes together as if orchestrated by some other force....

Anyways, I am trying, and I think failing to describe the type of magic that can happen when you let go and trust Spirit. Words can't do it justice. But trusting and letting go sometimes can produce powerful healing – just make sure you do this safely. All I did in the above example was choose San Pedro and the Redwoods forest as powerful tools for transformation - they did all the rest of the work themselves.

If you ever want to know how to serve yourself, serve others, or serve Spirit.... Be a hallow bone

Finding Our Own Ceremonies

"God writes the gospel not in the Bible alone, but on trees and flowers and clouds and stars." ~Author unknown, commonly attributed to Martin Luther

At this stage of our practice Tasha and I had a lot of excitement but weren't exactly sure where to focus it. We had just left the two mystery school cults and while we knew it was the only right decision to leave them, we also felt a little lost. We had a lot of programming from the two cults that we had to unlearn and rethink, and we really needed to reconsider a lot of our beliefs and perspectives on life in general. While some of the schools beliefs were wrong, they did build their fantasies on a foundation of some spiritual truths, so it was hard to separate what was real and what was a lie, and it was hard to tell what we were programmed to believe and what we really believed deep in our hearts. I especially felt very lost as I had been in these cults longer then Tasha. At this stage I had read so many books and taken so many classes on spirituality – most of them contradicted each other and so we didn't know where to look for guidance. We eventually decided that for a little while we just needed to explore on our own and spend a lot of time searching deep inside ourselves. In some ways we also had to let go of the comfort of knowing – and instead embrace living within in mystery and open-minded not-knowing.

I had taken a few classes based on core shamanism and read some books on the subject – I liked what I had learned there but felt that the school teaching these classes wasn't exactly what I was looking for. The practices and philosophies were a little bit watered down and I wanted something more specific and traditional. One thing about the core shamanism practice is that since the practices are stripped of all cultural ties, you can really figure out your own style to practice them in. There wasn't a specific way to open ceremony and close ceremony – you were encouraged to communicate with your personal spirit guides and ask them to help you design your own rituals and style of working. Most of the work was actually done on your own outside of class – learning directly from your spirits. So there was a lot of room to be inspired and figure out what works for you.

To try and develop skill with this practice we started trying to journey almost every day – like a daily meditation. We also started connecting with plant medicines again. Before the mystery schools and my focus on meditation I had experimented with many different psychedelics but for some reason after that 3 year break and after becoming more interested in shamanism we felt called to only work with plants – no more chemical substances. We also felt called to do our ceremonies in nature and to really focus on connecting a lot more with nature. So while we were at home we focused on practicing journey work with the drum and rattle, but we also started planning frequent camping and backpacking trips to do plant medicine ceremony deep in the woods.

We made our own ceremonies and found a format that worked well for us. Over time we simplified or changed parts of this format, but the format we were developing seemed to help us go much deeper with the plant medicines and helped connect us to the other nature spirits all around us – in the rocks and the trees and the clouds. The ceremonial aspect of how we connected with the plants really changed the effect they had on us and heightened the quality of the experience.

Our first attempt at working with plants in a more ceremonial fashion happened in the redwoods. Tasha and I were almost 2 years into our relationship and neither one of us had been to the redwoods before. Most of our camping had been at festivals and while we had done some other camping on a few occasions, we were mostly new to deep hiking and camping. I remember everything about this trip ended up working perfectly – we went for 12 days and had the best time ever.

The second day of our trip we wake up in the forest to a herd of elk that have surrounded us. We are at the Elk Prairie Campground in the Prairie Creek Park of northern California. We had a 12 mile trail planned which starts by hiking Miners Ridge, then a short hike up the beach to Fern Canyon where we take another trail called James Irving back to our campsite in a giant loop. This was April 2nd so it was early in the season and almost no one else was camped there – the trails were almost empty so we had tons of privacy.

We started the trail and early on we came to a spot that looks like a sort of theater – a big fire pit, a small stage area on the dirt and a bunch of seats facing the stage area. We decided to start our ceremony here. We sat and prayed for a little while, and then we called in the 4 directions in our own way – we spoke words from the heart and rattled to each direction while also burning sage to each direction and giving a small pinch of tobacco as an offering to each direction. We also called on the Earth and on the sky, and the 7th final direction of "here" was given to the spirits of the forest all around us. After calling in the directions we smudged each other with the sage and gave one final offering of fruit, grains and tobacco to the earth. Then we danced our animals – we started rattling, dancing, singing and making all the sounds that wanted to be expressed – we really let ourselves go and opened ourselves to our spirits. We felt alive with the energy and felt a deep connection to the forest in our hearts.

We then prayed one more time – calling on all our spirit guides, asking for blessings for our ceremony and asking the forest and land around us to bless and join our ceremony. We had mushrooms for this hike that we wanted to work with, so we held the mushrooms in our hands together and prayed over them – sending them all our gratitude and love and asking for healing and guidance. We stated our intention. We ate the mushrooms and started our hike.

Very quickly we started to feel the effects of the mushrooms. The whole forest came to life and everything was talking to us – the trees had faces and wanted to teach us. The earth cradled us and protected us. Every second of the hike was pure wonder and mystery as the spirits really opened up to us – we had both had many psychedelic experiences and other meditative and spiritual practice based experiences – but nothing like this before. This was something new for us – like we had entered into a new level of our lives and practice.

Every time we would turn a corner in the trail or get to the other side of one of these massive trees we would find new surprises. A new insight or revelation, a new spirit would appear, a new tree would surprise us, or a rock or feather would appear as if left like a gift... It is impossible for me to explain how magical the whole experience was – something that you really had to experience to appreciate, but if you have ever had a very powerful entheogenic experience in nature you may have some idea what I am talking about. To this day this is still one of the most magical experiences of my life.

At one point we top a rise and as we are finally able to see over it we both spot a tree in the distance. The tree was glowing and stood out from all the other redwoods – it looked as if faces and people and animals were swimming up and down its glowing bark. We both looked at each other without saying a word and somehow both knew we were seeing the same thing. Without a word we both started sprinting towards the tree and when we touched it – we both left our bodies and experienced a vision together. We were in this eternal loving light with God, and somehow this tree was God or God was in this tree…. And the tree blessed us and married our souls together for eternity. The experience was true unfettered love and bliss. When we returned to our bodies we were both sobbing tears of joy and had somehow ended up both sitting against the tree holding each other and crying…

I looked at Tasha and said "Did that tree perform a ceremony on us?"

"Yes, I think it did…"

"Did that tree just marry us?"

"Yes, it did."

We looked at each other both not fully believing what had happened or that we had both had the same exact vision and experience. We felt deep in our hearts that the tree had shown us the truth – we were really together sharing something special. We left an offering of tobacco for the tree and after enjoying its company decided to keep hiking.

Soon after leaving the tree I heard Tasha's voice in my head – like her spirit was speaking directly to me. Tasha and I shared everything, but there had been one secret I had kept from her – I was too scared to tell her or anyone else… But her voice in my head said "Travis you need to tell me the truth. You need to ask my forgiveness for this secret and you need to tell me the truth – but don't worry.

I will forgive you. You need to tell me. If you don't tell me, we will fail as partners and you won't achieve your dreams, but if you trust me and tell me the truth we will always be together and we will make our dreams come true together."

The secret had been burning me up inside for a couple months now.... As Tasha and I got closer I wanted to make sure there were no secrets between us. I wanted us to hold nothing back and really know each other. But I was frightened my secret would scare or hurt her.

I asked Tasha to stop walking and I started crying – I held her hands and told her I needed to ask for her forgiveness. I told her what was going on for me and she instantly without hesitation forgave me and supported me. I felt this huge weight leave my shoulders and my tears became tears of joy as we embraced – I had never felt so liberated before and I started to think that together we could make it through anything.

We kept hiking to a bridge and for some reason on this bridge we both fell over at the same time, caught each other on our way down, and fell on our backs laughing and crying as we saw a vision of a child above us – our future child. We knew we would have a child together and its spirit was saying hello to us – asking us to bring it into the world. I had never thought too much about whether or not I wanted kids before, but the joy I felt at seeing this image was so powerful I knew.

The whole hike was amazing and full of too many stories to share them all... But we were so touched by the special tree that we decided to go back and visit it every year.

Turning a Hike into a Ceremony

The last chapter gives you many details of our original hiking ceremony, but there are some more details in case you decide to try this one out for yourself. Immersion into nature is powerful medicine and when you bring intention and awareness into the equation you can really do a lot with this style of work. This type of ritual is something Tasha and I stumbled into together and which quickly became one of our favorite ways to do ceremony together when it is just the two of us. This ritual especially works well when you are camping or better yet backpacking – the deeper your immersion into the wild and the further you can get away from other people the easier it is to go really deep with this work.

In the last chapter I described an experience where we used entheogenic medicine to deepen our ceremony. You do not need any mind altering substances to do a hiking ceremony – they are optional. My experience is that the plant medicine or fungi can help you go deeper into the ceremony and they can be a great addition to the hike if you are experienced with them. One thing to be aware of in case you do decide to include entheogens into your hike – you should have some experience camping or hiking before adding entheogens just to make sure you are safe and prepared, and the plants or mushrooms will likely be stronger in this setting then you are used to. The combination of adrenaline and endorphins from the hike, seclusion in the wild, and the natural magic of the forest can really add some strength to these medicines.

Of course before starting this hike you want to do a little planning. Make sure you have a trail planned, or if not using a trail that you understand navigation skills well. One benefit of a trail is that you can focus more on the ceremony then the navigation as you just keep following the trail and don't have to put as much thought into it. Make sure you have enough liquids to stay hydrated, and unless you decide to fast make sure you have some food. Even if fasting it might be wise to have a snack with you just in case you need it – especially on longer hikes.

If you go backpacking and do this I get the best results by hiking in for 1-2 days, and then setting up a base camp that I can do a day-hike from. This allows you to get in deeper past the crowds at trail heads and gives you the experiencing of deeper immersion and waking up in the forest – this helps you go a bit deeper. The seclusion also means less distractions from others and the forest often gets wilder when you are further from the trail head. I will have all the food I need packed, camp set up and food secured in a bear canister or bear line, and the tent and weather protection I need will be all set up. I will also have a small day bag I can take on my day-hike from the campsite so that I can carry water and some snacks with me. The less you have to think about setting up camp the more you can focus on your ceremony – less distractions often means a deeper ceremony. Often a backpacking trip with a ceremony hike might look like 1-2 days hiking in, then 1 day of doing a day-hike from camp with the ceremony, and then a day of hiking out – a 3+ day trip is ideal (you can do any length trip you want though).

Once you have all your preparations for camping and hiking done you can focus on the ceremony. I may begin the ceremony at camp or I may start the hike and begin the ceremony at a nice spot early on in the hike. Generally you want to have some sort of intention for your hike – something you want to heal or let go of, or maybe something you want to understand or get insight on... Your intention can become an anchor for your ceremony that you can return to if your mind wanders and it also sometimes creates a framework for understanding any confusing messages you get during the hike.

You can open your ceremony any way that you like, but you should have a definite start to the ceremony – some type of opening ritual or prayer. In the example from last chapter we made an offering, called in the directions, connected with our spirit guides, prayed and set intentions and even smudged each other. You can add more to your opening or do less, or even do something different – this is your ritual. But make sure you have some type of opening – it really helps a lot. Often times we do a simpler opening these days – we may call in the directions, pray, and set an intention, then hike. Sometimes when we go backpacking I try to pack as light as possible and will leave things like rattles at home. Normally I use a rattle to call in the directions, but if I leave it at home I may just wave a branch I find that feels right to each of the directions – waving the branch and saying something as simple as "I call on the winds of the South and the Spirits of the South to open and bless our ceremony" can be a fine opening (if you don't have your own opening). Of course you would repeat this to each direction in a clockwise manner. Offerings at some point of the ceremony – either the opening or the middle somewhere can also be great. If you are including medicines as part of your ceremony – such as mushrooms or San Pedro or other entheogens, usually the best time to take them is after you open the ceremony.

Once you open your ceremony and ask the spirits around you to bless your ceremony – Creator, Mother Earth, the spirits of the forest or river or whatever nature you are nearby…. You can begin the hike. Start walking and slowly let yourself get lost in the hike. Hold the intention that by the end of your hike you will have found resolution for your intention – you will have found the healing or guidance that you seek. Long hikes are best to make sure you have enough time for this to happen – and you also need to trust that the medicine will come to you and embrace your hike fully. This can be a good time to practice the walking meditation from the start of this book. This can be a good time to really slow down and experience each detail of the forest. Touch the trees and hug them. Let them speak to you. Sit by a river and meditate – let the sound of the water drift you away into a dream like wonder. Listen to the wind and the birds. Let your heart speak to you and go with the flow – if you see a random excursion to try or feel drawn to something along your hike embrace your feelings and inclinations.

Play an interactive game with the forest – when you feel inspired by something near you play into it and let yourself get lost in the drama. Let the forest around you become this interactive adventure and ceremony – if you do, the forest will present opportunities that really bring out the magic of this experience. You may recall the example from the Hallow Bone chapter about telling one friend that if he climbed through the hallow log he would be reborn on the other side – this is exactly what I am talking about. Or maybe you find a river and decide to do a ritual washing of your hands, or maybe a lake or hot spring can become a place for a ritual bath and cleansing. Maybe you find the perfect spot for a break and meditate in between 3 giant cedar trees or on top of a cliff looking out over the landscape. Maybe you even see a more challenging side-adventure and decide to embrace your primal nature and get dirty or wet climbing over obstacles. Maybe you even cover yourself in mud to become one with earth. You can climb high in a tree to sing to the clouds or you can get butt naked and feel the liberation and freedom of the warm sun on your skin. There are endless opportunities in the forest if you go with the flow and are creative and open to inspiration.

When you are climbing up intense inclines and it feels like you are just pushing one foot after the other struggling through your hike – this can become a parallel to the way internally you are pushing through and working through your emotions and confusion and healing. This can be an opportunity to challenge yourself and as you overcome the hike you can also overcome your inner challenges and other challenges of life. You feel strong and powerful.

When you find beautiful rest spots you can sit and have some quiet. Listen to the forest. Enjoy the view. Think about life. Maybe even take a moment to do some other ceremony – shamanic journey, a nature mandala, meditate, yoga, make music... Perhaps even make an offering or smoke ceremonial tobacco. Or sit and focus inward – really pray for your intention. Feel your heart bursting with the emotion of your prayers. Sit down on the earth and feel the mother under you supporting you. Maybe take out a journal or sketchbook. Whatever your heart desires.

If you have never tried it before I also recommend attempting to barefoot hike at some point. You can do this ceremony with shoes of course, but going barefoot often adds an extra dimension to the ceremony – just make sure you don't over-do it if you are new to walking barefoot. If the ground is fairly soft and it isn't too cold out going barefoot can really make the hike much more enjoyable and adventurous feeling. As the sounds and sights of the trail change you can also feel the earth change under your feet. You have a direct connection to Mother Earth and also can ground ions from your body. Your feet get used differently and this is great for the muscles of your feet – the rocks and sticks can create a reflexology type sensation for you. You may even connect more with your primal self and attempt adventures you might skip with shoes – for example, many people wouldn't cross a stream that would soak their shoes, but if you are barefoot there is no issue getting your feet wet and you can maybe access parts of the forest you might skip otherwise.

Enjoy your hike and make the most of it. Let yourself connect with the spirits of nature all around you. When you finish the hike you may feel like doing some sort of closing ceremony – at the least I suggest expressing gratitude the beautiful land all around you.

Working With Plant Medicines

Then God said, "I give you every seed-bearing plant on the face of the whole earth and every tree that has fruit with seed in it. They will be yours for food." ~ Genesis 1:29

Entheogenic plant medicines are a true gift from God. An opportunity for healing, for deep insight about the self, or for finding and rekindling your connection to the spirit world and God. Working with plant medicines takes a lot of dedication and thoughtfulness – it is not something to play around with. These are very serious medicines and powerful teachers – and they deserve respect and care. In no way are plant medicines necessary for a spiritual path or for finding your connection to spirit – this is just the best and most effective way I know, and the only way that has really worked consistently and reliably for me. So feel free to make your own decision about whether or not working with plant medicines would be right for you.

If you decide to work with plant medicines you will have to decide whether you want to sit with a guide or engage the medicine on your own. I highly recommend a guide if you want to get the most out of your ceremonies. A guide not only keeps you safe, but they can also help you go deeper with the medicine and if they are good can help you receive the most therapeutic benefits from your time with the plants. We have talked a lot about the psychological and emotional healing done with plant medicines, but there is also an energetic component that is hard to learn on your own – this energetic component can change a lot about the experience and is only really accessible to someone with lots of experience and practice.

However, some people may find that they don't have access to any good facilitators. Maybe you do not know any local groups offering these medicines and cannot afford to fly to South America to work with shamans, so you decide to try things on your own. This is a totally viable option. Obviously if you have read this story, this is how I started out and it worked well for me though there were some ups and downs as I found my way. One thing I want to say though – after 7 years of intense study and practice using only my own experience and whatever I could read online or in books – when I first sat in a real ceremony with a shaman leading – I went deeper than I ever could on my own and experienced healing that had previously eluded me for years. There is a substantial difference between being in a guided ceremony versus being on your own and you cannot really compare the two experiences. They are on such different levels that it is really like talking about two different things.

This guide here is for people who feel called to connect with plants on their own, and especially for people who may want to use some of the rituals in this book inside of a plant medicine ceremony. For those serious about working with plant medicines I also recommend the more thorough books which I wrote that is focused solely on plant medicines and their different uses: The Plant Remedy.

Of course I will not be able to cover all entheogenic plants here, but since the first step towards working with these medicines is choosing a plant to start with I will give a quick overview of the most popular choices as well as my recommendations. If I was going to recommend one plant first to people it would probably be San Pedro. San Pedro is a cactus originally from Peru and Ecuador that now grows all over the planet. I think this is one of the safest and easiest plants to work with on your own, and as a bonus, in many countries it is also very easy to obtain as it is a popular ornamental plant. In USA you can buy, sell and own San Pedro without breaking any laws (though it would technically be illegal to make medicine with it as this would involve extracting mescaline). San Pedro is often described as heart medicine, or heavenly – it has such a small dark side compared to some other plants, and can be a great intro to plant medicines because it starts you off by building a foundation of light and love before you go into any darker plants. I also see people grow and heal very quickly from this plant – it goes straight to practical advice and healing and people can get powerful results with less difficulty then some other plants require.

The second medicine I would probably recommend isn't technically a plant at all – magic mushrooms. These are any mushrooms which contain psilocybin (there are many varieties and while slightly different, they are similar enough to lump together). This is another medicine that for many people could be easy to obtain and is fairly easy to work with – most places you have options of foraging for them in the wild, or picking them from cattle farms, growing them at home from legal spore kits or finding them from a friend who has them. The mushrooms do require a little more care though, as they can sometimes be a darker or more confusing medicine compared to San Pedro – this darkness isn't bad as it is the mushrooms bringing up your shadow so you can heal it, but if you are not prepared to handle it you could be in for a difficult time. San Pedro can also bring up your shadow, but usually in a gentler way. One benefit of working with mushrooms is how easy the dosage is to control – each species of mushroom has a general relative potency, and once you have discovered the right dosage in grams of the mushroom you can easy dose yourself to the correct level. Other medicines like San Pedro or Ayahuasca may be harder to figure out the exact dosage from batch to batch because they can vary more in potency. Generally mushrooms are a very insightful and powerful medicine and they are relatively easy to work with (they happen to be my personal favorite).

Ayahuasca is a very popular plant medicine these days because of recent media exposure. It is a great plant medicine, though I don't always recommend it as much as the above two for people working at home. There are two main reasons I usually recommend other medicines first: the Ayahuasca is more complicated and harder to learn on your own, and it also takes more work and time and sacrifice to get to the same depth as you can with other medicines. It is not that other medicines take you deeper – it is just that the Ayahuasca is often much more work. It is harder to understand, harder to prepare, you usually restrict your diet and lifestyle to work with it, many ceremonies might be light or seem like nothing happened because it is less predictable and more easily blocked by other energies ect.... There are a lot more variables in working with Ayahuasca compared to other medicines. This doesn't mean you cannot work with Ayahuasca on your own at home though! If you really feel specifically called to Ayahuasca you can learn to work with it by either sitting with a guide, or putting in a lot of time and work and starting off with real small doses then slowly working your way up.

There are also many other medicines you could work with from the plant and fungal kingdoms. Amanita Muscaria is a wonderful mushroom different from the ones mentioned above (it does not contain psilocybin – it contains ibutonic acid and muscimal). Salvia Divinorum is a plant with powerful visionary medicine (also legal in many countries and fairly easy to work with). Morning Glories and Woodrose (both contain LSA similar to LSD) are another option, though I have limited experience with these. Tobacco and cannabis if used in a balanced and moderate ceremonial manner can be powerful allies. There are also other medicines like iboga, datura and yopo. For the type of work that goes along with more rituals in this book though I think most people would benefit from mushrooms, San Pedro or maybe even cannabis or tobacco. Medicines like Ayahuasca or Salvia are often better indoors or in a private location where you can focus on just the plant. Sometimes Ayahuasca is okay outdoors in the day or at night around a ceremonial fire, but for simplicity we will focus on mostly uses for San Pedro or magic mushrooms for this book. If you feel called to look into other plants I refer you again to my other book The Plant Remedy.

I feel that most plant medicine ceremonies fall into two categories: indoor and outdoor. Indoor ceremonies are usually done at night with as little distractions as possible to help facilitate an inward journey. They can be in silence or with music, on your own or with a shaman leading the ceremony. Sometimes there may be minimal lighting from a candle, but often times for these ceremonies the darker you go the better. The darkness allows brighter visions with more clarity, and the dark silence creates less distractions so it is easier to go deeply into yourself and focus. This is a good way to do deep ceremonies.

Outdoor ceremonies are usually done in nature and because this book focuses on ways to connect with nature we will focus here. A couple details that help you make the most of your outdoor ceremony include choosing a spot that feels safe and accessible to you, and also choosing a spot with as much privacy from other people as possible. Other people can be very distracting and can bring in unexpected energies into the ceremony – you really want to focus as much on yourself and the plant as possible during ceremony, so the distractions from other people are not really desirable at this time. Complete privacy is nice, but not required – just enough privacy for you to feel comfortable and be able to focus.

Once you have chosen a plant to work with and researched it enough to feel confident hosting your own ceremony you can get started. With San Pedro you may have powder, a tea or juice, and with mushrooms you may have just the straight mushrooms to consume, or you may have them prepared into a tea or other food like chocolate. I personally like to have the mushrooms prepared in 2 gram chocolates so that it is easy to measure dosage without any scale. Before beginning your ceremony it is nice to have all plant medicines prepared ahead of time so that on the day of the meditation you can focus solely on the ceremony and not worry about as many practical details. In fact, as many practical life details as you can get out of the way, the better – it is best if you have the entire day free to focus on just your ceremony. No phone calls, no visitors, no driving, no cleaning or other work – try to do as much of this before ceremony as you can, so that you can have your mind free of other obligations.

For ceremony you need to consider your set and setting. Where will you be consuming the plants? Are you planning on being stationary or moving around a lot like a hike? If hiking – are their break spots early on in the hike where you can have a bit of privacy to meditate while the medicine is "coming up?" These break spots can be very helpful in case you need to stop to focus on the medicine or in case you get overwhelmed and need a break – if your hike can be flexible there is a greater chance of going deep with the medicine. Sometimes walking and hiking helps you go deeper, and sometimes you really need to sit and focus, or stop and deal with something in the ceremony. If some past trauma comes up for you to heal for example, it may be hard to focus and work through your emotions fully if you don't sit down and take a break (in some cases you may find the walking helps though – it can change from day to day and you never know what kind of day it will be until you are in it). A plan that lets you be flexible and embrace the needs of the moment is best – of course sometimes you have to work with what you got.

You also need to think about whether you will be doing your ceremony on your own or with someone else. Usually the smaller a group is the more you can focus on yourself – so smaller is generally better for going deep in ceremony. One exception to this is when you may need a sitter or facilitator – someone to watch over you or guide you, or just be there as a back-up. If you do have a sitter I often think it is best if they stay as hands-off as possible, unless they are trained as a ceremonial guide. Go into the experience thinking you will be responsible for yourself, but just in case you have a friend there who can help calm you down if you get overwhelmed. People can get themselves in a fix trying to host ceremony for someone else and pretending to be a ceremonial leader before they are qualified, but being a sitter who just offers support and calming words or a hug can be a way anyone can help. If you have an experienced guide who is more than a sitter, then they should know how and when to help and you can probably follow their advice as long as it seems reasonable to you.

If you do a ceremony like this with friends it is important to make sure before starting the ceremony that you are all on the same page. If you don't talk about this beforehand you may find yourself in a situation where you want to meditate and work through your healing, but your friend wants to talk and distract themselves all day.... And if that is the case it can be easy for you both to walk away frustrated from an awkward experience. So if you want to do a ceremony and focus inward you should discuss this beforehand to make sure your friend is interested in the same thing. There is a difference between ceremonial and recreational use of these medicines but not everyone knows or understands this difference – so it is best to be proactive about this and figure out these details before starting. If there is no guide or facilitator I would also recommend mostly giving each other space, but just checking in with each other occasionally. Don't put yourself in a position to be their "healer" but if they seem to be struggling ask if they want to tell you about it or if they want a hug if you feel called to do these things. But don't push anything on them – in many cases people need time and space to work through some of this stuff and if you try to help them too much you can actually distract them and pull them away from their healing. You may find that you need to just let them cry something out while you give them space. Offering support in the least distracting way often helps the most, and sometimes giving them space and trusting they will work through things can be a great way to support them. Of course if they ask for your help and you feel up to it – there is no harm in a few kind words or a hug.

When you work with plant medicines there are generally a few different sections of the day or the experience... Before starting the ceremony it is common to feel nervous and sometimes this may make you emotional. After ingesting the medicine is a period many people call "coming up" on the medicine. This coming up phase can sometimes be the most difficult or scary because everything is changing so fast. This part can also sometimes be very exciting and blissful – be careful that you don't take a second dose too early just because you feel great and think more would be even better..... Wait till you finish coming up to decide if you want more. With San Pedro it often takes 2-3 hours to reach your peak and I have seen it take up to 5 hours before, and with mushrooms it generally takes about 60 minutes. Sometimes people don't feel very much at first – especially if they get too in their heads trying to control the experience – this is another reason to wait till you peak before ingesting seconds because you might have a slow come-up and not realize how strong it is at first. Understanding this come-up phase of the medicine and preparing for it can help you set up your day to flow better. The most helpful consideration here is generally making sure that you have a good location for this part of the experience just in case it is more intense then you were expecting.

At the start of the ceremony I also like to have some sort of opening ritual. For me the minimum ritual here would be praying for a good ceremony and setting an intention for the ceremony. Your intention can be vague or specific and can include more than one thing, though there is only so much you can fit in a ceremony so no need to list every possible intention you can think of. For a prayer I like to express gratitude first and then ask for protection, healing, insight and whatever else I feel is appropriate – I think prayers are best coming from the heart in the moment and usually skip reciting memorized prayers. If you feel like you want a little more ritual then just the prayer you can add anything else you want – an offering, calling in the directions, pre-ceremony smudge with sage or other herbs, journaling, yoga, or any other ritual you want.

During the middle phase of the ceremony after the come-up is the peak of the ceremony. This is usually when the medicine is the strongest and also when it often talks to people the most. The peak can be easier or harder than the come-up depending on the day and the person. Sometimes it is easier because you have adjusted to the altered state of the medicine, and sometimes it can be harder if the medicine shifts and takes you into some trauma healing. Also expect the medicine to come and go and shift in waves – you might start to feel like you are sobering up when suddenly another wave of the medicine hits you and takes you in even deeper than before. Generally a single dose of San Pedro will include 1-3 hours coming up, another 4-6 hours of peaking, and then a long and slow settling or coming-down phase for a total ceremony length of 10-15 hours. Mushrooms usually come up real fast – about 30-60 minutes, and also come down real fast at the end – total ceremony length is usually 5-6 hours unless you extend it with a second dose. If you feel like you are sobering up before that amount of time, don't be surprised if you get hit with another wave of the medicine – give yourself some time relaxing before deciding that you really have returned to baseline.

Remember also that this is a ceremony and that it might involve difficult work. Many people have a natural reaction that when they don't feel good they either try to run from the feeling or fix it. This can be detrimental in ceremony sometimes. For example, maybe in the middle of ceremony you shift from feeling this blissful oneness with nature to suddenly feeling very sad and alone. You may try to repress the sad feeling or ignore it, but if you do you will miss a chance for healing, and chances are if you try to repress these types of things in a plant ceremony that the plant will not let you repress it. These medicines have a way of exposing you to your own truth and a way of bringing up the past traumas and repressed emotions you need to heal – so chances are sudden emotional feelings or memories are actually something repressed coming to the surface to be healed. So the best thing you can do in this case is actually embrace it and go into the uncomfortable feelings so that you can work through them and process them. Ask the medicine or God for support. Pray. Remind yourself that this is what you wanted what you asked the medicine for, and that it is only temporary – you will work through it and feel better once it is processed. Things can get more uncomfortable if you try to fight your own healing – asking the plants to expose your repressed self so that you can know it and heal it, but then trying to keep it repressed in the moment ends up turning things into a mini battle with yourself and battles with yourself aren't really fun.

After the beginning and middle parts of the ceremony you eventually come to the winding down phase of the medicine. Things start to calm down and settle a little bit. The effects start to fade. In many cases after the mushrooms wear off you will feel pretty close to sober unless you are smoking cannabis or adding other plants – adding other plants or smoking cannabis will make the mushrooms linger for a bit and last much longer (which is not always desirable, but can work well if you plan for it). San Pedro usually lingers until you go to sleep in my experience, but it does mild out quite a bit. This section of the ceremony is good for making sure you remember the lessons from earlier in the day – take some time to write down things you may forget, or if you are with someone else you may wish to talk to them about your experience to help yourself understand it better. This may also be a time for heartfelt connections if you are with someone else – if you spent the previous parts of the ceremony focused on yourself, now may be a good time to bring the group back together to connect. You can make powerful connections with friends, family and partners with the plant medicines, so this can be a really nice phase of the medicine. This can also be a time to eat some food, rest, or maybe do a little grounding or cleansing work. At the end of ceremonies I often like to use some sort of smudge like sage or palo santo, and often times I will also work with a little tobacco for cleansing and clarity as well. It is nice if your ceremony has some sort of closure and a final smudge can be a great closure. Other ways to close might be with a prayer of gratitude for your ceremony, a song to close ceremony, or maybe you want to give thanks to the directions if you called them in at the start of your ceremony.

Smudging and Soplada's

For thousands of years people have been burning different plants and herbs for their medicinal benefits and mind altering abilities. Shamans, monks, priests – they all use burning herbs as part of their ceremonies and rituals. This smoke can have many different benefits all at once. The smell can help you enter an altered state and can facilitate calmness, inner peace and clarity of mind. The smoke also has anti-fungal and anti-bacterial properties in many cases – so by smudging a sick person you can actually be helping them in a very physical and measurable tangible way. The smoke can also be a powerful manifestation of the plants spirit (the plant you are burning) and can also be a medium for other spiritual forces – like your own spirit guides and allies.

There are many plants you could smudge with and many different methods you can use for smudging. Some of the most popular and common plants include sage, cedar, juniper, palo santo, sweet grass and copal (there are many others, this is just a few). Some people also use blends with many plants or use incense. My favorites are usually white sage and palo santo, and sometimes copal. Some of the methods you can use for smudging include just burning regular incense or loose incense/resin with charcoal or burning loose herbs in a bundle (like sage or sweet grass). You can just let the smoke diffuse naturally or you can direct it by waving around the burning incense itself, or by using feathers to "fan" the smoke. The smoke is often used for purification and for blessings and can be used on participants, on the room or space the ceremony is in, or on the medicine itself. I find you get more energetic benefits from the smoke if you pray when you use it and set an intention.

Using feathers to fan the smoke works really well and is probably my favorite method. You can use any feathers you find naturally or you can purchase a special feather fan – a special fan or special feather might even have its own energy that you can connect to and which can permeate through the smoke. If you remember the chapter where we talked about hallow bone work and letting spirits work through you then you might have an idea how you could call on a spirit to work through you as you do smudging work. An example of this may be that I have some eagle feathers in a blessed fan and also have an eagle spirit ally – well I might invoke that eagle ally to work through me and manifest its power through the action of the fan and the smoke in my hands. In this way the eagle medicine has a powerful medium to manifest its influence on the recipient. If you really let this spirit manifest through you there may even be a chance you will experience seeing the energy you are clearing with the smoke and know where and how to use the fan and smoke – you may even have songs or prayers come through you from the spirit.

Besides fanning the smoke you can also smoke it with your mouth and then blow it onto people. In Peru where I have spent a lot of time studying they call this a sopla. Basically any small outer cleansing can be a sopla – they might blow smoke, fan smoke, spray floral water from their mouth or do a flower bath or anything like that. You could use herbs like sage for this still, but I use mapacho (Amazonian tobacco – Nicotiana Rustica). Sometimes I may even mix a little sage into my tobacco for added effect. In this smoking and blowing method you can use rolled cigarettes (not chemical tobacco or anything like that, but hand-rolled with nice ingredients), or you can use a pipe. A ceremonial pipe may be blessed and have its own energy similar to a feather fan. For this you might begin by whistling or blowing a prayer into your smoking blend – tobacco works especially well for this as tobacco is really easy to program with intentions. Then you can breathe it in and blow the smoke onto the recipient while also blowing your intention with the smoke. There are some shamans who can heal just by blowing tobacco on their clients. Often times this smoke is blown for protection, blessings or cleansings.

If you want to spray floral water from the mouth you can also provide cleansing and protection or blessings this way. This is very common in many shamanic traditions. It also looks very impressive and dramatic (nothing wrong with enjoying what you do!). In Peru they mostly use Agua de Florida for this (scented floral water – basically a combination of really strong alcohol, perfume and herbs). The Agua de Florida has a nice effect and energy but I personally don't like the chemical ingredients so I prefer to make my own floral water by soaking some herbs in alcohol, straining them out, then watering it down and maybe adding some essential oils if I feel called to. There are two methods I know for spraying this water. The first involves just taking a swig into your mouth and then forcibly spraying the water out through your top teeth while jutting out your tongue a little bit (hard to describe in a book, but if you find a YouTube video of a shaman spraying someone you might be able to imitate them). The second method is greatly preferred – instead of taking a regular swig you first make a pocket in the front of your mouth by pushing your tongue against your bottom lip – then you just pour a tiny bit of the liquid into this pocket instead of all the way into your mouth. You blow it out the same way. The second method is preferred because the floral water does not taste so great and because the high alcohol content can sometimes burn your mouth a little bit. Just like with the smoke you can blow intentions with your breath when you "sopla" or spray someone.

With floral waters sometimes I even just see people rub some on their hands and then over their bodies, or I see people put just a little in their hands for smelling. This is an easier and more gentle way to sopla yourself. It is also possible to put the floral water in a spray bottle and spray it around as a type of smudging – some people also do this with rose water and essential oils in water.

Make Your Own Agua de Florida

Since I mentioned making my own floral waters in the last chapter I thought I would include a recipe or two here. Feel free to make your own recipes as well.

The basic method for making the floral water starts with getting high proof alcohol – preferably 100 proof or higher, though something lighter also works. Something with less scent and flavor might be best – potato vodka is an easy choice. Choose what herbs you want to include and soak these herbs in the alcohol – I usually soak them for 1-3 days. Afterwards strain the herbs out and you have basic floral water. I personally like to take mine a step further though – I like to water down the alcohol at this point (after soaking the herbs) so that it doesn't burn so much and I usually like to add some essential oils if I didn't have all the herbs handy that I wanted to use. I also like to add some prayers to my water and sing to it – maybe even blow tobacco smoke on it. With the herbs strained out this water should store for a long time because of the alcohol.

This is the first recipe I ever came up with when I first wanted to try making my own floral water. I soaked fresh picked lavender and dried sage in the alcohol. Once done I then added peppermint essential oil, lavindin oil and a "thieves blend" of essential oil (thieves contains: clove bud, lemon, cinnamon bark, rosemary and eucalyptus essential oils). Sage has a cleansing and protecting energy as does lavender – lavender also destresses and helps you relax. Lavindin is similar to Lavender and provides a similar function. Peppermint helps you focus and clears the sinuses. The thieves blend is great for cleansing and protection. So this recipe was mostly geared towards protection and cleansing but also has a soothing and invigorating quality to it. It also smells great. Because of the alcohol and antibacterial function of some of these oils – you can even use this blend to clean surfaces or clean your hands!

Here are a few other herbal blends for you to try which have different focuses. Some are more floral and uplifting and some are more cleansing. You can use the herbs you have available to you or use essential oils for some of the herbs if that is more accessible.

Try mixing bergamot, neroli, lemon, cloves, cinnamon, lavender, rose and orange flower. Or try ylang ylang, lemon, lavender, sage and rose. Another option might be rose flowers, jasmine flowers, cinnamon sticks, mint, lemon balm, basil and thyme. If you want a super cleansing brew perhaps try a little mapacho added in with sage, palo santo, cinnamon and clove (go light on the mapacho for better aroma). And of course – feel free to experiment with your own recipes as well!

Cleansing Baths

Another great way to give yourself a cleaning similar to smudging or sopla is to make a ritual bath. This can take on many forms and there aren't really any rules here so don't limit yourself to only my suggestions!

Did you make Floral Water from the last chapter? Why not add some to a bath! Or maybe you didn't make the floral water but you do have some of the same herbs – add those herbs to your bath directly and soak in them. If you already have scented bath products those can work as well – preferably use ones without chemicals though. If you have natural plants added to the water you can pray to those plants for their healing and blessings as you bath.

Flower baths are found in different cultures and traditions. In the Amazon before ceremony a shaman may have you bath in Ajo Sacha (for removing evil and sorcery) or perhaps bath you in Guyasa (for blessings and good energy). Rose water can be amazing to bath in. Or even a simple mix of rose, sage and lavender for a relaxing, cleansing and heart opening bath.

It is also very helpful to add salt to a cleansing bath. Salts act as a purifier and help ground your energy and cleanse you. Epsom salt works especially well but you can use any salt in a pinch. I prefer Epsom salts, dead sea salts or regular sea salt. You can add the salt to the water with the herbs and then just soak in it, or you can even rub some of the salt on your body while you shower to help cleanse your superficial energy (what some might call your aura).

You can do a ritual bath quickly or take your time. In the Amazon we would soak the plants in water for a bit and then splash the water over your head with a bowl or bucket – almost like a hand shower. You would splash your whole body and that was it. But if doing this at home with salts and plants in the tub it can be very nice to soak for a bit and relax – go for the full experience and consider some candles or relaxing music as well. Really feel the tension, stress and energy you no longer need seep out of you. When you pull the drain imagine all that unwanted energy you let go of washing down with the water – let all that energy go and really consciously think about it going and see it going to get the best results (don't do the bath habitually, but do it intentionally and with awareness).

Bathing in natural waters like hot springs, a waterfall, a river or a lake can also be incredible. Icey waters like a glacial or alpine lake can be very powerful and cleansing – not only the spirit of the lake adds to this, but the temperature therapy is great for your immune system. This can be a great way to connect with different nature spirits – communing with the sacred waters.

More Practice With Shamanic Journey

At this phase of our practice we were still learning a lot on our own. Because of the bad experience we had had with previous schools and teachers we decided working on our own for a while would be best until we really found someone worth studying with. I did take a few classes on core-shamanism with the Foundation for Shamanic Studies, but mostly we just spent a lot of time in nature meditating and connecting, doing a lot of our own plant medicine ceremonies, and we also practiced our drumming style journey work at home. The drumming style journey work was interesting, because after a while Tasha and I both found it easier to journey without the drum. Sometimes we would feel called to use the drum or rattle, but many times we had great results just using visualization.

This journey method helped us a lot during this phase of learning – it was safe and easy enough to practice on our own at home, and the main focus of the practice is really learning directly from your spirit guides in the journey – so having lots of practice helped us learn more from those spirits. Often times before and after plant medicine ceremonies we might do journey work to help understand and integrate the plant medicines better. When we had personal issues we usually journeyed to tap into our inner guidance on how to set things straight. We also wanted to improve our skills so we started some exercises to help us develop deeper in our journeys.

We already covered one of the basic healing practices with shamanic journey – power animal retrieval. This is a good basic start for people who need it – a way of reclaiming a lost connection and lost power. There is lots of other healing work you can do with journeys, but two of the main energetic components are often called extraction work and soul retrieval.

Sometimes when we experience trauma or are overburdened with stress, our bodies and energy fields become open to outside intrusions – outside energies that want to combine with you or even feed on you in certain ways. These intrusions are spiritual or energetic in nature, but may result in physical symptoms. And Intrusion can be like a curse, or just invasive energies from emotions and thoughts, some type of energetic pollution, or it can even be a spirit. Even when it is not a spirit the energy can sometimes take on a consciousness of its own and start to act like a spirit – almost as if it develops its own sense of self preservation. When someone has an intrusion for a long time they can also become attached to it in some ways – like a familiar friend that isn't really good for you, but that you are used to and comfortable with. So in removing this energy sometimes you really have to deal with the intrusions desire to remain, and even the client's fear of change and letting go. Extraction work is used in many spiritual healing practices – it can be performed with plant medicines in the form of a purge, or it can be accomplished within a journey itself, or it can be done through hollow bone style work like we discussed earlier in the book. Generally if you are performing extraction on someone else one of the main guidelines is to first fill yourself with power – this is a spirit that fills you with strength and works through you guiding the process, and the best way to know what spirit to use is either to ask your guides for a volunteer while journeying, or to learn a specific method from a skilled teacher.

The first method of extraction work that I learned was using the hollow bone method and calling in a power animal who protected me and worked through me to perform the extraction. You start to enter your altered state with drumming or dancing or your other preferred method, and you start calling in the spirit until you feel filled to bursting – if you have room for fear then you need to call in the spirit more. Call in the spirit until you feel like you are filled with power – until you are "power-full." Let the spirit guide your work – some shamans do this with sucking or with plants or smoke, or they may use tools like a phurbas or bronze mirrors, but the simplest method to use is your hands. Start pulling the heavy energies you see off of them with your hands and give that energy either to the earth, a large body of water, or to a fire. It is important to give this energy to something that can transmute it because otherwise it will hang around and just attach to someone else. So you pull the energy from them, send it back to something else that can transmute it, and then you fill the space with new energy – you can fill the space with a power animal retrieval or soul retrieval, or you can send in positive light energy or positive plant energies ect…. You want to fill the space the intrusion was in, so that the person is no longer open and inviting to other intrusive energies.

It is also important to protect yourself and cleanse yourself when doing extraction work. This is why you have a spirit work through you – the spirit is protecting you as it works and you are engaging the negative energies less. You might even notice energetic gloves or maybe even the "hands" of your spirit guide glowing over your hands while you do this work – so only the energy and spirit is touching the intrusions, not you, because you have that layer of protection. When using a power animal for the extraction you may see things like feathers or claws over your hands, or feel called to use your hands and arms as if they were wings. In some traditions the practitioner even uses sacred objects for the extraction work – maybe sacred feathers or a feather fan like used for smudging, or a phurbas or bronze mirrors, or plants. Tasha does excellent extraction work using plants she will gather from wherever we are in nature and brush away energies – the plants will tell her which ones to pick and use and how to use them and she just trusts her intuition like described when hollow-boning.

While performing extraction work you may feel called to sing or hum or you may want to have an assistant drum for you. If you can channel medicine songs you may be singing away the intrusive energies, or you may be singing to connect with your spirit guide who performs the extraction through you. The songs can also protect you. Having a drummer can really help you enter a better trance. If you have a rattle this can be a great tool for extraction because you can use the rattle to break up energy intrusions that you want to pull out – you can shake the rattle over energies that are trying to hide as a way to sort of smoke them out, then you can get at them better with your hands or extraction tool.

Soul retrieval works very different from extraction work. When we experience trauma, sometimes our soul or psyche protects itself by separating away the traumatized part, and hiding it. In other words - we repress or block off parts of ourselves that are painful for us to engage, and when these parts of ourselves become repressed we do not heal them and they can manifest as different illnesses or challenges. Soul loss often leaves a feeling of incompleteness or separation from yourself or from spirit, and sometimes it leaves a hole to be filled (which may result in addictive behavior). Using different techniques, pieces of the soul and psyche can be found and reintegrated into the whole, which often brings healing and comfort. In some cases people describe this as a piece of the soul separating from itself and getting loss, which is where the term soul retrieval comes from, but this is just the way the energy looks in journeys – really this is something repressed and hidden away in the psyche.

Soul retrieval can be done in many different ways. Plant medicines often perform this type of healing naturally as part of their experience – they bring up repressed emotions and traumas to be worked through and reintegrated. When doing this through journey work though it is best to have this intention to do soul retrieval and to practice and develop skills that facilitate this type of work. In a journey sometimes your power animals or other spirits might perform a spontaneous soul retrieval on you and help you, but when journeying for others it is most helpful if you have developed a lot of skill at journeying, because you will need to really trust the messages and visions you get to be effective, and that skill is how you can ensure the safety of your ceremony.

When you journey to perform soul retrieval you begin with your intention. From here you may feel guided to do an upper world, lower world, or middle world journey. Most people do lower or middle world journeys for soul retrieval. If you are unsure where to start I would start in the lower world – if it is the wrong spot to start then one of your guides should redirect you. Start searching in the journey with the aid of your spirit guides to find the "lost" parts you need to retrieve – take as much time as you need. Sometimes there are obstacles to overcome before you get there – maybe confusing twists and turns, or other spirits trying to block your path even. You will need your spirit guides and your discernment to navigate to the source of the issue. When you find what you are looking for it could really look like anything. It may be an object or it might even be a memory or event…. I often see the client as they were when the soul loss happened – so often a little child lost or alone or scared – depending on what trauma caused the soul loss. When I see this child or person in the journey in most cases I needed to talk to them and comfort them and help them feel welcomed back to the "whole." Basically this is a part of someone that has become repressed and alienated from the rest of that person and needs to be reintegrated. Usually comforting love and compassion as well as empathy and understanding are what starts the process of reintegration. You really have to follow your intuition and do your best here – because each situation is unique I cannot give you a recipe to follow to make this work – you must trust yourself and your guides to find a way. Often times I will retrieve and hold this lost shard of the soul once it has been comforted and take it out of the journey with me the same way I would when retrieving a power animal – then blow it back into the person (the crown or heart are often good spots, but trust your intuition where to blow it back into). If possible do some work to comfort the person outside of the journey and help them reintegrate this part of themselves back. Talk to them about the journey and see if you can both start to understand what happened and what can be learned from the whole process.

Along with any healing service like this it is always good to talk to the client afterwards. You want to help them understand what caused the issue in the first place, and also understand what can be learned and gained from the difficult experience. Trauma and suffering are never pleasant or desired, but they are a part of life and we benefit most by making the best out of any situation we find ourselves in – in this case learning and developing into stronger more compassionate people is the gift found in our suffering. Difficult times and challenges help us develop our character and if we focus on learning from our past and from our suffering we can stop the trauma from controlling us and move on with our lives in the best possible way. Learning to face our own fears and trauma can help us develop courage and maybe more importantly – helps us develop empathy for others. When you go deep into your past and your trauma you will find how much your suffering shaped your decisions later – how you may have even hurt others because you were suffering yourself. But you were always doing your best – you just had so much pain that you became overwhelmed and overburdened. But as you accept this about yourself and begin to forgive yourself – you start to see that other people around you are also doing their best and if they hurt you – chances are they were acting out of past trauma themselves. It doesn't excuse anyone's behavior, but it does help us have understanding and compassion for each other.

When we face ourselves, and face our past and our suffering.... We begin to slow down and even stop the patterns of the past that keep reliving themselves. In this way someone who was abused as a child can treat their own children better and stop the cycles of pain. Someone sexually abused can help council other victims and help stop their cycles from being repeated. We can stop repeating the mistakes of the past by learning from them. What could be more healing?

Journey Practice

If you want to get more skilled at journey work there are some things you can practice to help develop and test your abilities. These are helpful for gaining more experience and are especially helpful for learning soul retrieval work. Soul retrieval work can sometimes take a little longer to learn mostly because you have to get very reliable information from your journeys in order to find the lost and repressed parts of someone.

The first exercise to practice with involves journeying back to something that happened earlier in the day involving someone else. Pick a specific event from the day that seemed important to you and journey back to it. The reason you want this event to involve another person is so that you can check with them afterwards as a way to validate your journey and see how accurate you are. A perfect opportunity for this might be you having a conversation with a friend and feeling like there was something left unsaid, or you felt like something was troubling them or occupying their mind. Within your journey explore what was left unsaid, or what might have been on their mind – then the next day you can check with your friend to see how accurate you were. This works best if they do not know till afterwards that you were going to journey about them, but make sure you also respect people's privacy and try to pick someone you think would be open to you working with them this way.

The second exercise can be a fun one – hide and seek with a friend. Choose a partner for this one and ask them to imagine themselves somewhere – anywhere they want. It can be somewhere from real life or from a movie or story. Ask them to imagine it as deeply as possible and really see themselves there. Then do a journey and try to find where they are at – try to describe what it looks like to them and see how accurate you are. This is a skill that develops with practice so don't worry if it takes a few tries – but you may also be surprised how often you get this right. This exercise is especially helpful for learning soul retrieval work, and you will have to find parts of someone that are hiding, just like you have to journey to find where your friend is hiding in this activity.

The third game to test your accuracy is to choose a store or public place you have not visited yet and do a middle world journey there. When you find the place in your journey try to get a basic idea of the layout of where things are and what they look like. Focus especially on bigger more solid and permanent things, as little details might change and move….. After your journey you can go visit the location and see if things were laid out similar to what you saw in your journey there.

I have some other ideas for personal journey work that can help you practice and help you learn about yourself. These are just a few ideas to get you started and to hopefully inspire more ideas for you.

Asking your guides about your habits can be insightful. For example, you can journey to the upper world and ask your spirit guide to show you circumstances when you tend to give away power – notice the habits of why you give away power sometimes and find ways to recognize when you are doing it later in life. You can also journey to the lower world and ask your power animal to show you a song or symbol or charm that you can use to defend yourself against giving away your power when under the above circumstances. Another good idea is to journey to your inner child and see where they are neglected and how you can bring them into your life more, or journey to past traumas or life changing events to learn more about those parts of your life and how they still effect you today.

When you want to learn new practices, like shamanic extraction work, you can journey and ask for a spirit to volunteer to teach you and help you with that work. Or you can ask your current spirit guides to introduce you to a spirit that does that work. Or if you have new tools you want to use in ceremony – like a rattle, feathers or a new crystal, you can journey to a spirit that can teach you to use those tools. You can hold the tool while you journey and they might even show you by using the tool through you! You can journey to spirit guides and ask them to teach you new songs for specific issues you are having – like protection, or opening the heart for example, or instead of songs maybe they will teach you something like symbols or dances instead.

You can journey for advice in your life. If you aren't getting along with someone you can journey to the root cause of the issue and find out how to resolve it. If you have a difficult choice to make you can journey to find out what your heart says about the matter. When you have health issues you can journey to the affected area in your body and see if there is any insights to help you get well again. If you want to learn about chakras or work with chakras you can journey into each of your chakras and see how they are feeling and what they have to tell you about yourself. If you have specific goals you want to accomplish you can journey to find inspiration and make a plan for how to bring those goals into reality.

If you want to learn new rituals and ways to work with medicine you can journey about it. Journey to find out how to open and close sacred space or how to call in the directions. Journey about how to structure your plant medicine ceremonies. Journey to learn about your weak spots in protecting yourself energetically and how to protect yourself better. If you have a client asking for help you can do a journey first to see what services they might need and see what work you can do to help them.

With just these few examples hopefully you see how many ways there are to use your journey work, and hopefully you are inspired with ideas of your own to work on.

Past Lives

I don't know if past lives are real, but I have had a few experiences that I thought were past life experiences and they were very insightful. In particular I want to share an experience I had while learning some more advanced journey work.

I was working for a teacher who taught shamanic journey and Q'ero mesa altar work – she taught at a local college and I was her teaching assistant for a year. One day in class she told people to do journeys to the upper world and ask their guide to show them 3 past lives: the life where they suffered the most, the life where they had power and did the most harm, and the life they had power and did the most good. I decided to journey along with the rest of the class and see what answers I could find.

When I asked to see the life where I suffered the most I was transported to the Holocaust in Germany. I was in an internment camp and as soon as I realized where I was I felt a deep fear and sadness come over me like I had never experienced before. As soon as that wave of feelings hit me and I realized where I was that part of the journey ended very quickly – it was as if it was so horrible and scary that I could only experience that one brief moment of it…. Even from that single moment I felt how horrible it was and knew how much I had suffered in that life.

Then I saw the life where I had power and did the most harm. Interestingly enough I was Jewish in this life as well – but this time I lived in ancient Israel and was a member of the Jewish royal family. Somehow I knew this was about 3000 years ago and that it was around the time of King Solomon. Being a member of the royal family I had a lot of power – and while I had good intentions I made mistakes and mislead my people in a way that has had ramifications into the present day state of that region. I felt a deep shame and regret and saw how quickly the mistakes of someone with so much power could hurt so many people. I also realized how much our actions can affect the future – even thousands of years later.

The third life I saw was when I had power and did the most good, and this is where I spent the most time in this journey. Somehow I knew that I was in the region of modern day Turkey and I felt like the time period was about 13,000 years ago. Each life was going further back in time. In this life I lived high in the mountains and I had a garden full of datura and would often forage nearby for Amanita Muscaria mushrooms. I grew many other medicinal herbs in my garden as well. In this life I lived with someone I knew was the same as my mother – but in this past life she was my sister instead of my mother and we lived and worked together. We were healers who offered many types of herbal treatments but specialized in shamanic style healing with Amanitas and datura. We did a lot of dream work as well – which is interesting because these two medicines are very helpful for dream work, but I did not know much about these medicines at the time I had this journey. In this life I had power from the spirits instead of the power of the royal family and I used my power to help people heal and grow instead of making political mistakes that misled people.

These three lives at first may seem kind of random, but as I thought about them together I realized they taught me a lot about myself. I saw how these three lives really represented a lot of my current fears and desires. Because I have Jewish ancestry I can relate to the Holocaust visions – my family had to flee that same Holocaust in the 40's which is why my family came to the USA. Any time I learn about the Holocaust I can really see myself there, because that was my tribe being persecuted and my family was deeply affected by that event. A part of me also fears persecution for my current spiritual practice – at any time I could be thrown into a mental hospital against my will and be restrained and drugged if I told the wrong person that I talked to spirits. Or I could be arrested by police even though I am practicing my sincere religious beliefs by working with plant medicines. Where I live my spiritual practice is demonized and persecuted so I could relate in many ways to the vision I had of my past life.

I also saw that in the second life where I had power and did harm that I feel aversion to situations where I would need to make decisions for others. I love being in control of myself, but I never feel like I know what is best for another person. I don't like being a part of large organizations in this life, and maybe that is related to how bad being a part of a large government in that didn't work out so well. Some of my poor decisions in those visions were related to religious beliefs too and I have always had a lot of skepticism about large religions – in my experience they often mislead many people.

In many ways I see myself trying to create the life where I had power and did good. I feel a deep connection to living in nature and working with plant medicines. I want to help people find joy, inner peace and health. I think if I can integrate the lessons from the other two past lives I could add that to the knowledge I had in this particular past life and really shine in the present reality.

Putting these three lives together really taught me a lot about my inner fears and desires. If you feel like you are proficient at journey work then asking to see these 3 past lives for yourself could teach you a lot. I don't know if the past lives are based in reality or if they are just a vision from your heart designed to teach you and provide insight – but I do know there is a lot to learn about yourself here.

Vision Questing

"We know that God is everywhere; but certainly we feel His presence most when His works are on the grandest scale spread before us; and it is in the unclouded night-sky, where His worlds wheel their silent course, that we read clearest His infinitude, His omnipotence, His omnipresence." ~ Charlotte Brontë, Jane Eyre

Since we are discussing how to connect with spirit guides in the modernized core-shamanic way I thought we should also explore a traditional way to connect with your personal guides. You have probably heard of vision questing and you might have some ideas in your head about what it is from movies or books, but the traditional way it is done by North American Natives might surprise you and be a little different then what you expect. Each tribe does their style of vision questing a little bit different, and I am not going to teach one specific tribes style – I am going to teach a simplified but effective style that anyone can do. This style is based on the central practices and requirements of what makes an effective vision quest, and while each tribe adds a lot of their own customs to this practice, they all have this foundation in common.

The first step is to decide how long you will quest for. This is partly based on how comfortable you are fasting. Since you will be doing this on your own without a teacher watching you or a community supporting you I recommend staying on the shorter duration of 1-5 days maximum. If you are not experienced with fasting do not start at 5 days – start with one or 3 at the very most and work your way up. I have heard of some tribes questing as long as 21 days which is super hardcore – but they worked up to this level gradually and they also have a teacher making sure they are safe and usually their community is doing ceremony to send them energetic sustenance while they quest. If you find a legitimate group that you can quest with you can certainly do a longer quest with them if they think you are ready.

Some people like to start their fast before they begin the actual vision quest so that they are deeper in the experience during their quest. This can be very helpful – but like I said before, you need to work up to long fasts. You cannot just do a long fast if you don't have any experience with them – this can be dangerous.

The more you fast the more your body becomes used to fasting and the longer you can safely fast.

Fasting can be an extremely rewarding practice when done safely. In moderation it is great for your health – studies show that fasting can revive and strengthen your immune system and fasts have been known to cure many illness's and ailments. If you haven't researched fasting at all I suggest looking into it before trying this practice just to make sure you understand what you are getting into and how to be safe. Research might also get you more excited about fasting once you read about all the benefits to your health and life. If this is your first time fasting you may also wish to try a 1 day fast or juice fasting first, or experiment with intermittent fasting. Juice fasting is when you skip all solid foods and only drink fresh squeezed vegetable juice – this can be a good warmup to try before doing a full fast. Intermittent fasting is where you only eat one or two meals a day instead of 3+ meals. So with intermittent fasting for example you might only allow yourself food from 2pm-6pm each day while fasting the rest of the day (this practice is based on only having a 2-6 hour window where you allow food).

For vision questing you should do a full fast. Some tribes allow you to drink water and some require a fast from water as well – you can choose which way you want to quest if you aren't questing within a specific tradition with a teacher. I recommend allowing yourself water if it is you're new to fasting, as fasting without water is much harder and can be more dangerous. I would prefer fasting with water allowed anyways.

To begin your quest you must first choose a spot in nature where you will have privacy and no one will bother you. Don't choose a spot on a trail where hikers will walk by – choose a spot that is hidden. It doesn't have to be hidden far away, but it is best if you only see and hear nature during the quest and don't have any outside distractions. Once you pick your spot you will want to mark out a square around yourself using the 4 directions. Eventually when you start the quest you will not leave this square except to use the restroom nearby, so pick a good spot that feels right to you. To mark out the 4 directions you could use rope or something but I prefer to use natural objects like sticks or stones. I also like my "walls" to face the 4 cardinal directions of north, east, south and west and think this is a good guideline to follow as best as you can (so that your quest includes the medicine wheel). Make sure this space is large enough for you to lie all the way down in so that you can sleep, but you don't need it much bigger than that. One point of this is that you will be sacrificing and showing dedication by remaining in this small space for the entire quest, so a space just a little longer then you need for lying all the way down is usually perfect. I would say at the most the spot could be 10x10 feet. Make sure there is also a good bathroom spot nearby (you don't have to poop in your tiny square, don't worry!).

You won't need many supplies for this and if you feel up to it, it is possible to do this with no supplies, though that could be very hard. Generally it is considered good to bring minimal rain cover and enough to keep yourself warm, water if you are allowing water during your fast, and nothing else. Some tribes do have the quester make tobacco pouches or ceremonial arrows or something like that – if there is a specific spiritual focused craft that is part of your quest, of course that would be allowed as well. A good minimal set-up might be a single tarp tied up as rain cover and a sleeping bag and pad to keep you warm at night. Generally you would have no fire, though I don't know every tribe's traditions and some might allow this.

So once you know how many days you will quest, and have picked out and set up your spot, you can start the quest. Usually you will eat nothing the day you start and some people even fast a day or two beforehand as well. You mark out your directions, get inside and once you start your quest with a prayer you do not eat any food or leave that spot until the quest is over. Do not end your quest early unless there is an emergency – pick a duration and stick to it. Do not leave or eat any food until you have finished the quest and closed it with a prayer.

Prayer and dedication to the quest are important. You want to really pray from the bottom of your heart and mean what you say. Feel your prayers. Feel the emotion within them. Pray for the spirits to come and trust as much as you can that they will show up at some point if you stay dedicated to your quest. Pray for healing, pray for insight and guidance. Pray for connection. Pray to be of service. Pray. This is the main point of your quest – to pray and to listen.

Do not distract yourself during the quest. No reading or listening to music. Don't practice music even – though you can sing medicine songs and prayer songs to help your quest. Don't bring an instrument at all though – this is supposed to minimal and it's just you and the spirits! Nothing else! No sexual activity. No electronics besides maybe a flashlight for at night. Just sit in your spot and pray and wait.

Some tribes have specific activities they might do for part of the quest – in some traditions there may be a special stomp or dance that you do over and over. Some traditions might have you make ceremonial arrows or tobacco pouches like I mentioned. These are spiritual activities that are part of the quest, but you don't want to distract yourself with other activities. You don't really want to exercise for example, but you can do some light pacing or stretching so you don't get too stiff, and if you feel there is a ceremonial dance or stomp you want to do that could be beneficial as well. Don't bring a craft to distract yourself with, but if you are making a ceremonial craft as part of your quest that is fine – just don't use it as a distraction!

During your quest things might get hard. You might have extreme emotional pain, extreme physical pain, sickness, doubts…. This is something you have to pass through to prove your dedication as part of the vision quest. It is not an easy ceremony, but it can be very powerful. If you stay dedicated the spirits do appear and there is nothing subtle about it.

This can be a very powerful ceremony and is best when used during transitional periods, or when you have very important questions or prayers you want answered.

Engagement

"Where your treasure is, there also will be your heart" ~ Paulo Coelho

Tasha and I had been dating for a couple years now, and we were really becoming close with our joint interest in spirituality and healing. Relationships in their own way can be a powerful medicine and tool for personal development – we lived with each other and spent almost all of our time together. While we were inseparable and deeply in love, sometimes we would get on each other's nerves just because we did absolutely everything together. Something about spending so much time with the same person really exposes you to your own shadow – when you can no longer hide your shadow from the person you are with it also becomes harder to hide it from yourself. So spending this time together really reflected to each other our true natures. We would rarely leave each other's side except to go to work. Mostly though, things were going very well between us.

I remember the first time I realized how much she meant to me. About 4 months into our relationship Tasha became pregnant. This was a surprise to us and when she first told me I kind of freaked out – I had no experience with children, didn't even know if I wanted them, and our relationship was so new to me still…. But at the same time I didn't feel good about having an abortion or anything like that, so Tasha and both knew we would be parents together. The day after she told me I had some more time to process and think things over – and I suddenly realized how much I really wanted a child and that I wanted it to be with her. She was a nanny and daycare teacher and would make the most excellent mother – and I had never met another woman who appreciate me so much and tried so hard to treat me well. I finally saw how special she was and how much I loved her, and I quickly became very excited, though still nervous about being a dad.

A week after discovering we were pregnant Tasha had a miscarriage. She was only 5 weeks pregnant but it was still a tough emotional blow to us. On the bright side we both knew we would be better off waiting to have a child, and now that we both knew we wanted children we had become much closer together as a couple. We were disappointed but also glad that we would have more time to prepare and get ready to have a child sometime later in the future.

A few months later we went to the Redwoods for the first time and had the magical experience with our favorite tree. We kept growing closer and closer together. In some ways we felt as if that tree had married us, though we mostly kept that little miracle to ourselves.

Later that year after our redwoods experience I applied for a free trip to Israel called Birthright. If you are one quarter or more Jewish and between the ages of 18-26 you can apply to attend a free 10 day tour of Israel with a group of people your age, and I wanted any excuse to travel. With my interest in Kabbalah I was also excited to see Jerusalem and Tzefat and the rest of what Israel had to offer.

I had known about the Birthright trip for a few years, but I had thought the cutoff age was 25 and I was 26. I was working at a spa in Seattle as a massage therapist when I met a new co-worker one night. I had never seen her before, but it was her last day at work and she had booked a "going away" massage with me. As I was massaging her I noticed she had the Hebrew letters for the word "Chai" (which means "life") tattooed on her left wrist. The letters that make up the word are yod and heh. I told her how interesting it is that we have similar tattoos – because I had the 4 letter name of God tattooed on the same exact spot: yod-heh-vav-heh. My tattoo had the same two letters, and just two extra letters. She was excited to meet a fellow person from the "tribe" at work and told me how she had just gotten back from her Birthright trip and had totally loved it. I told her how sad I was I had waited too long and missed my chance to go.

She asked how old I was and when I said 26 she was excited to tell me I could still make it if I applied right away. She gave me the website to apply on, and I applied that night when I went home. It is funny how these synchronicities work because that was the last night registration for the next trip was open – and the trip was the last possible one I could attend, because it started just a few days before I turned 27 and became too old for Birthright. So a co-worker I had never met just happened to get a massage from me on her last day of work, and just happened to have a matching tattoo on the same part of her body that led to her telling me about Birthright the very last night I could ever apply before becoming too old. I turned 27 on the last day of my trip in Jerusalem.

Israel was an incredibly magical experience for me. There is a deep magic and powerful energy in the land that was very palpable as I traveled. I was also in a Birthright group that focused on outdoor adventure so we had a lot of time to really connect with the land. We camped without tents under the stars in the Negev desert, we floated in the Dead Sea, we went cave crawling and repelling off cliffs, and we did many hikes. We of course also spent time in cities like Jerusalem and Tel Aviv and besides traveling with 8 Israeli soldiers so that we could connect with locals, we also stayed 2 nights with Bedouin Muslims in their desert tents. It was a very powerful and transformative experience for me – something about the land, the history and the people really brought up a lot of emotions inside of me.

In the middle of my trip we visited a city considered the birth place of Kabbalah – Tzefat. This is a beautiful small mountain community above the Sea of Galilee. I went walking by myself around the city and as I was looking at a jewelry store I found a special ring I wanted to get for Tasha. It was a Hamsa with prayers of protection carved into it and a little diamond (Hamsa is the symbol of a hand with an eye in the palm found in many religions). I didn't think about the associations between diamonds and marriage at the time, but one of my friends on the trip pointed it out to me and joked Tasha would think we were engaged if I gave it to her.

I decided then that I would propose.

I got back home the night after my birthday on Christmas Eve. The next morning Tasha and I went on a long walk by the beach and I asked her to marry me – she said yes! We didn't tell our families right away though – for some reason we felt like we wanted to focus on making a dream come true before focusing on our marriage – we felt the need to visit Peru.

That morning we also did a ritual together – a letting go ritual with the ocean.

Letting Go Ritual

Tasha and I would often create little rituals of our own using nature to help us heal and grow. Many times these rituals would be like little acts of drama and theater to help us work through emotions – when you play along and let go of your critical mind you can actually open yourself up to magic in almost any act.

For this ritual Tasha and I did a long walk by the beach in Seattle. We talked about our relationship and all the things that blocked us from achieving our deepest connection together. We talked about all the things holding us back that we were ready to let go of. Talking about these things was a good way to pull all those blockages to the surface and find a vulnerable and open frame of mind conducive to our ceremony.

You do not have to be in a relationship to do this ritual – anyone can do it. You just need to have something you are ready to let go of. You can journal about all the things you want to let go of and how they affect you and appear in your life or you can just think about them and imagine them in your head. This is an important step to really put a name and a face to what you are banishing so to speak. Just like the way plant medicines might show you your trauma to help you work through it, you really need to look at and experience a little bit of what you want to let go of to get the best results.

When you are done with that part of the ritual walk down the beach and let your intuition guide you. This can be a beach by the ocean, or by a lake or river. Water is powerfully cleansing and nurturing and adds a nice effect to the ceremony. Let your intuition guide you where to walk and guide you to an object you can put your pain and troubles into. It can be a stick or a rock or any natural object that is easy to throw. When you find it, take as much time as you need to put all the energy of what you are releasing into the object – feel it flow out of your hands into whatever object you chose and think about everything you are letting go of. Let it all go.

When you feel like you have given everything you can to the object throw it as far as you can into the water. Feel everything you put into it leave you. Watch the object sink and be washed away. Feel the lightness of letting go of that baggage. Say goodbye.

You may feel emotional releases while you do this, or you may feel a need to cry. The more you let out your emotions and let yourself be vulnerable the more this ritual works. If you want to you can keep walking to have some time to think about what you let go of and how much lighter you feel now, or you can write down anything you want to remember in a journal.

Our First Trip to Peru And San Pedro

"One day you will wake up and there won't be any more time to do the things you've always wanted. Do it now." ~ Paulo Coelho

I mentioned earlier in this book that when I first got interested in psychedelics and saw them as healers and teachers, I also started to read about Ayahuasca. I had experienced a number of synchronicities that made me feel as if the Ayahuasquero's and healers of the Amazon had something important to teach me – it was the first time I had ever heard of a tradition still alive that used entheogens for healing and mysticism, and many of them described the same exact visions that I was having at home. For a long time I was not able to make it down to the Amazon where this medicine is available – I did not have enough money for travel like that, I didn't' know any reputable healers to stay with (and had heard horror stories about the bad ones), and I had also gotten distracted with the two mystery school cults that I fell for. After 6 years of reading about Ayahuasca and knowing I needed to make it to Peru sometime, I finally found the circumstances to make it down to the jungle. My dream was really coming true.

By this time I had gone deep into studies with psychedelics on my own, I had spent a number of years meditating and doing ritual, I had worked with mystery schools, learned energy work, and practiced all kinds of mysticism and other spiritual practices. These practices had brought me a lot of joy in my life and they had helped me know myself on a deeper level than I ever knew possible. I had found a personal connection with Spirit and become increasingly certain that my path laid in healing – I thought about healing and mysticism all the time and it was my greatest passion. I had gone to massage school and was working as a massage therapist while also doing energy work for people on the side, and at this time I had just finished publishing my second book on spirituality and healing.

Tasha and I were having a powerful time connecting with nature and getting back into plant medicines. The one struggle we had trouble shaking though was our finances – we were living in the woods with a couple good friends but we struggled to make ends meet... We did have access to affordable plant medicines so we were getting deep into our practices at home and doing a lot of self-discovery. At this time I was reading a book called The Hummingbirds Journey to God which is about San Pedro cactus. I had worked with San Pedro a few times in the past on my own – it was actually one of my favorite plant medicines to work with, though it was a lot of work to prepare and at the time I didn't know how to make it very strong. Every once in a while I would feel called to connect with it again and would brew my own at home and go drink it in the woods on my own or with a friend or two. When I started reading this book about San Pedro I became much more interested in the plant. Before I had only read about Ayahuasca traditions using plant medicines for healing, and I had heard a little bit by this time about mushroom cults in Mexico or Iboga use in Africa…. But I had no clue that there was a San Pedro tradition in Peru where shamans used the plant in similar ways as Ayahuasca – for healing and guidance. As I read about the personal healing stories with this plant, the miracles and the ancient tradition of shamanism – I instantly felt a strong need to reconnect with this plant on a much deeper level. Something about this plant even started to call to me more than Ayahuasca did – and that was saying a lot! The book also focused on a few specific healers in Peru and I became very interested in them – especially the San Pedro shaman called "La Gringa" in the book who people reported healing paralysis, depression, cancer and all kinds of illness with.

So Tasha and I decided to make a big batch of the medicine with our two roommates at the time. We were brewing up a large pot of San Pedro when out of the blue a friend showed up at the house unannounced. This was a friend from the city, and we were not close to the city – we lived about an hour drive away and usually people did not just show up unannounced. So our friend popped in the door took one whiff of the brews aroma, and said "I recognize the smell!" He looked into the pot, "You guys are cooking San Pedro. How awesome! I drank a bit of that when I was in Peru a few years ago!"

I had the Hummingbirds Journey to God book sitting out and I grabbed it to show him, "Wow you spent time in Peru? I bet you would dig this book." I handed him the book and he started to flip through it.

He stopped flipping through the book for a second, "Wait a second, I know these people! I stayed with them for a few months, they are good friends of mine. Do you want their email?" He was pointing at a picture of La Gringa and her two sons. I finally had a personal connection to a reputable healer in Peru and I was one step closer. Before I didn't have any idea how to find a good healer to stay with, but now that was changing.

I talked more with my friend and he told me he also knew a few trusted Ayahuasquero's in Peru as well. The one he recommended the most was a man named Ricardo Amaringo who owned a center in Iquitos. So now I had a recommendation to visit Ricardo's center Nihue Rao, and to visit Lesley Myburgh (La Gringa) in Cusco. As the pieces were coming together I was becoming increasingly motivated and felt like I needed to make this happen. Tasha was on the same page as me – she had some healing she wanted to do, and I had some learning I wanted to do, and we both felt that Peru and plant medicines was the best bet. The plan was coming together, but we still did not have the finances to make it happen. I thought about Peru every day and felt something tugging on my heartstrings – I knew we had to make the journey happen soon.

Just at this time when our plan was coming together things were getting pretty hard for Tasha and me. We moved back into the city of Seattle but we both lost our jobs at the same time and we owed our roommate a month's rent that we were behind on. Money was real tight. At this time our roommate told us the landlord was going to raise rent in about 4 months and we didn't think we could afford it, so we decided we needed to move. For some reason I had this undeniable conviction that when we moved we needed to turn it into an opportunity to make Peru happen. I knew the plane ticket to Peru was expensive and I didn't know when we would be able to make anything like that happen again, so I thought we might be able to put all our belongings into storage and save money by not having rent to pay while we traveled – I hoped that this would allow us to travel longer and make the most of our trip down there. As this plan came together Tasha and became dead set that no matter what – we had to find a way to make it to Peru when our rent went up. We consciously dedicated ourselves to this goal and decided to find a way to make it happen.

As soon as we became committed to a specific time to travel everything shifted. Before we had been waiting for the resources to manifest before planning our trip, but this time we just decided we would force them to manifest if we had to. We somehow both got new jobs right away and paid back our roommate, and started saving up really quickly – I don't even know how this was possible since our jobs did not pay very well. It seemed like we saved up more money than we logically should have been able to in that time frame. We also sold our nicer car and started sharing one old beat-up Honda I had had for years to add to our savings – I made the sacrifice of waking up early each morning so I could skateboard an hour to get to work each day instead of a ten minute drive. As the date approached we also found that we didn't need to put all of our things into storage – we found another friend who had an open bedroom in his small 2 bedroom apartment and we moved in with him so he could watch our cat while we traveled. Because 3 of us were sharing this cheap mini apartment we were able to keep our bills very low and had things in place so that we could travel.

To have enough time to travel as long as we wanted we both realized that we would have to quit our jobs. Our travel plans involved 2 months in Peru, and when we got back our families wanted to take us on family vacations, Tasha's family wanted to take us to Hawaii and my family was meeting in Utah for a reunion. After so long not traveling anywhere we suddenly had huge travel plans ahead of us like we had never experienced before. As we realized that we needed to quit our jobs to travel we decided to make the most of our time off from work, and we planned a cheap road trip down to the redwoods after seeing both our families – so we would have 3 months traveling in total before we returned back to working jobs again. Needless to say we were both extremely grateful and astounded at the opportunities in our lives. Things were really coming together, and while all the traveling would stretch our bank accounts to the limit of what we could afford, we were willing to rough it for a bit in order to make things work. For us, this was the chance of a lifetime.

We told our families we were going to Peru to work with plant medicines and described how we were going to sit with traditional shamans in the jungle, and they were pretty confused. To them the idea sounded crazy, "Why would you spend all your money drinking psychedelics in the jungle with some random natives you don't even know? Isn't that dangerous? Why do you need to do all these psychedelics?" My dad even researched Ayahuasca online and found an article titled "The Dark Side of Ayahuasca" that really freaked him out. They were pretty worried about us and tried to talk us out of it, but of course our minds were set. We knew that we would be safe and that this was going to be an amazing healing adventure. We had some fears too of course, but we couldn't let them stop us.

We first flew into Cusco to stay with La Gringa – Lesley Myburgh. Lesley was originally from South Africa, but after having deep healing experiences with San Pedro she had moved to Peru and did a traditional apprenticeship with a local healer. She originally learned all the traditional practices that most healers were doing with San Pedro, but some of those practices didn't feel authentic for her to keep doing – so Lesley and her teacher developed a different style of working to fit her personality and background better. She is one of the best known healers in Peru and we were excited to stay with her at her hostel Casa de la Gringa. She also has twin sons Mark and Simon who run a travel company called Another Planet Peru – so I had organized a whole tour with them for Tasha and me, and Tasha's dad even joined us for the first 10 days of our trip.

Right away we did our first San Pedro ceremony with Lesley at her house near Temple of the Moon. She lives just outside of the city of Cusco in the most magical place you could ever find – she has the most wonderful garden where you do ceremony, and after a few hours in the garden participants can go explore the countless temples that surround her house. Temple of the Moon is the most impressive – a deep cave that looks as if animals are growing out of the rocks. When you go inside the temple it feels as if you are entering a vortex of some kind – the air gets thick and heavy and gravity feels stronger. You can feel the energy so much that you can touch it. We were deeply touched by Lesley and her sons and the magic of her garden – both of us had very powerful ceremonies. Even though I had worked with San Pedro numerous times on my own at home, this was the first time I had met the spirit of San Pedro and it was like a whole new side of the medicine had opened up to me. Right away, with no doubts in my mind I knew San Pedro was the medicine for me. Of course, I was still curious to try Ayahuasca in a few weeks, but I was glad we started with San Pedro and I felt Lesley was the perfect guide to introduce us to the real power of this medicine.

I remember that night after the first ceremony with Lesley sitting around with the other participants from ceremony and eating dinner. We were all sharing our experiences from the day and lessons learned, and when it got to be my turn to share I replied something like "Oh, it was pretty gentle, not much happened... I remember feeling connected to everything, and lying face down on the grass, petting the Earth and telling her how much I loved her. Then I had all these insights about people in my life and how I could show them extreme and unguarded unconditional love and how to express that love and accept that love all the time."

Everyone replied, "What do you mean not much happened! That sounds amazing!"

I realized that while San Pedro had been very gentle it had also been very powerful and insightful. I didn't have these giant wild visions of a cactus talking to me or condors flying out of the sky to heal me – but I had deep personal insights and revelations. San Pedro had shown me such an extreme version of love that years later I am still scared to be that loving – pure unconditional love unguarded in any way. I hope one day I am ready to embrace that extreme level of love and expression, because it was beautiful. That being said – even though I couldn't bring myself to express the level of love San Pedro had shown me that day I did become a lot more compassionate and caring to myself and others and I did learn how to manifest a part of what San Pedro had shown me. I think ever since then I have been in a gradual process of learning how to be the version of me that I had seen through the eyes of San Pedro that day.

After the first ceremony we did some traveling to Machu Picchu, Ollantaytambo, Lake Titikaka and the Sacred Valley. I was extremely interested in ancient cultures, temples and ruins and megalithic structures, so this was amazing. Our guide Miguel that Lesley's sons had arranged for us helped us understand the local culture and really connect with the spirits of the mountains.

In many ways these temples have their own magic and it felt like visiting the sacred places of Peru was a ceremony in its own right. A few nights after our first San Pedro while we were in Aguas Calientes I even experienced San Pedro appearing to me in a dream and showing me a movie – I woke up and wrote enough notes that I could write a book later based on what I had seen. I had always wanted to write fiction – ever since I was a child. This dream became my first fiction – The Shadow Twin.

As we returned back to Lesley's house in Cusco after our travels, we did a few more ceremonies and really got to know the city of Cusco. We had a few weeks to relax there and really sink in. In some ways Cusco already felt more like home then anywhere I had ever been before in my life. The year before I was able to go on the free trip to Israel called Birthright, and I had felt a deep pull from my ancestors and the land there, but in a different way I really resonated with the culture and people in Peru – and of course the plant medicines were always tugging on my heart strings. We met many people who told us how the plant medicines had healed their illness and some of them we saw be healed with San Pedro in ceremony. We were very sad to leave Cusco, but we were also excited to go to the Amazon next and finally meet Mother Ayahuasca.

The last day that we sat with Lesley I was thinking about how powerful and beautiful her ceremonies were and how much I really wanted to learn healing like that. San Pedro whispered in my ear: "You know, you could host ceremony like this. Just trust me and I will guide you. When you get home share me with someone and I will show you – you are ready to host ceremonies with me."

I thought to myself "No way! This just must be my ego talking! No way am I ready to host San Pedro ceremonies!" I had been drinking San Pedro for about 5 years at the time and had been on my spiritual path for about 7 years, but I was certain I would need in depth training to safely host ceremony with a plant medicine. It must have just been my deep desire to eventually do this work speaking through my ceremony.

Ayahuasca and the Jungle

After leaving Cusco we flew into Iquitos. Iquitos is the largest city in the world not accessible by a road – you can only get to it by boat or airplane. It is also known as the tourist destination for Ayahuasca – people from nearby areas of the jungle will move here when they want to open an Ayahuasca center to serve tourists and there are literally thousands of Ayahuasca shamans around the Iquitos area. We were booked to spend two weeks at a center called Nihue Rao which was owned by a Shipibo shaman named Ricardo Amaringo as well as two westerners – a doctor from the USA named Joe Tafur and a Visionary artist from Canada named Cvita Mamic. They have a really unique center in that they work with traditional Shipibo practices, but can also help explain and share things from a medical perspective and they encourage a lot of artistic expression.

Even though we only took a little time on airplane to move from one part of Peru to the other, it was like a completely different country. The cultures and environment of the jungle is vastly different from the Andes Mountains. In the Andes people are very calm, humble and quiet, but also very helpful and welcoming. They also have numerous spiritual practices – some of them work with San Pedro or Coca, but many of the Andean healers do more energy work practices and work with mountain spirits, condor feathers, stones or offerings to provide healing. In the Amazon people are wild and life moves fast. Healers work with tobacco and Ayahuasca mostly. The jungle feels almost lawless and kind of like the "wild west." It is a very exciting place to visit.

Tasha and I are deeply into nature so we really appreciated the intensity, diversity and beauty of the Andes and the Amazon. In the Andes we loved the giant mountains and deep canyons with huge man-made temples that look as if they grew straight out of the rocks themselves. Quiet little villages with peaceful people toiling hard to work the land. The jungle has an intensity of plant and animal life all crawling over each other that is amazing – it looks as if all the plants are strangling each other and eating each other, and are in a constant state of death, birth, growing and decaying. In the jungle you can really see the cycle of life and death in vivid realism. We felt like explorers of some kind visiting these ancient temples and going deep into the worlds wildest and most massive wilderness. This sense of adventure and deep nature immersion was a powerful teacher and therapeutic tool.

When we got off our airplane Nihue Rao had a mototaxi driver waiting for us at the airport. Mototaxi's are motorcycles with a little rickshaw-type-seat on the back for passengers and are the main mode of transportation around Iquitos. They can be pretty wild to ride – the drivers don't stay within the lines and will drive straight at oncoming traffic swerving around each other at the last second. We were having a blast.

The drive to Nihue Rao took us two hours down a dirt and mud road – we were a little ways outside of the city. The road was in such bad shape that I often had to get out and push the mototaxi and many times the driver had to have us lean to the right or left trying to balance the bike as we went through giant puddles of mud. The jungle itself felt secluded and peaceful. We arrived at the center and were shown to our tambo's – little huts they use so you can be in isolation in the jungle. We set down our bags and got settled in, and then went to drink a purgative as a preparation before Ayahuasca ceremony. If you are not aware of the Ayahuasca tradition, it focuses heavily on purging as a way to cleanse the body and spirit. They handed us a big bowl of warm soup – it kind of looked and tasted like a strange version of French onion soup. We chugged it down and then sat waiting for the purge to start. At first we felt fine. After about 15 minutes or so you suddenly become very sweaty and hot and projectile vomit shoots out of you for a few minutes. I had never experienced anything like it. As someone who rarely puked in life and hadn't puked in years it was a pretty intimidating experience. I felt nervous and excited, and very sick.

Next we were introduced to Ricardo the shaman. I was expecting a smile and a handshake or maybe even a hug…. I thought someone working with plant medicines as a healer would be loving and friendly like Lesley was, but Ricardo was very distant. He wouldn't look me in the eyes. I became very nervous at first but then thought that maybe he is just in a trance state or looking more at my energy then our immediate surroundings. He seemed kind of somewhere else or in a daydream of some kind. I didn't know enough Spanish to talk to him so the other owner Joe translated. They asked what I wanted to work on and I told them I wanted to see if Ayahuasca was a path I was interested in learning, and I was hoping to get insights into my spiritual practice and learn more about healing. Ricardo kind of smirked at that – looking back I can see why, as even if you think you have done a lot of healing work before coming to Ayahuasca, Ayahuasca is going to give you a thorough cleaning! It takes years to learn anything about healing and I was only there for two weeks. Of course I wasn't expecting to leave a shaman or anything like that, but I know now that with plants it is best to start with personal intentions regarding yourself and your healing. Often times you learn the most from the plants by asking them to teach you about yourself.

We weren't just at the center to drink Ayahuasca – we were also planning on doing a master plant dieta. This is a practice with strong ties to the Ayahuasca tradition. Basically you go on a very restricted diet of green plantain bananas and bony river fish with the occasional potato or bowl of rice, but no salt, oils, spices, sex, touching other people, media, ect. You are also in isolation during the diet – hence the tambo hut. During this period you also choose one plant to focus on connecting with and while you are on the restricted diet you consume the plant every day and pray to it – asking its spirit to enter your body and heal or teach you. Because you are in isolation and on such a bland and nutrient deficient diet you start to become very weak and sensitive – so you really feel the influence of this plant spirit you are working with. Ayahuasca has a special role as a teacher about other plants, so often times Ayahuasca is used during the dieta to help you form a deeper connection with the plant.

So at this first meeting with Ricardo I was assigned a plant. I think because the intention for my visit to them was so vague they assigned me a plant based on my current line of work. I had mentioned that I was a massage therapist so they assigned me a plant called Suelda con Suelda which is supposed to teach you about a very intense but effective style of bodywork called bone setting. It is also supposed to be a heart-opening plant. After they assigned me my plant they asked Tasha to come in and assigned her a plant as well. She wanted to heal intense chronic back pain that had been troubling her for 3 years and was very emotional explaining it to them. After looking at her energy Ricardo said she was suffering from *susto* – soul shock or soul loss. They assigned her a plant called Pinon Blanco which is supposed to be good for connecting to light and heavenly energies and for healing susto.

That night was our first ceremony. They told Tasha to not drink the first night, but just come to ceremony so they could sing to her. They told me to start with just a small amount to drink since it was my first time and since I had done an intense purgative just a few hours before. One thing I really like about Nihue Rao is the recommend starting of slow and working your way up to help you get used to the medicine and find your proper dosage. I had heard horror stories about the taste of the Ayahuasca and about the scary visions and dark spirits that the shaman clean from people... I had no clue what was going to happen. Here I was lost in the jungle with no way back to town but the people I was staying with. My first time with jungle natives and they didn't speak my language. We were staying in a wild jungle with a million ways to die – jaguars, piranhas, snakes, poison plants, spiders and frogs, malaria infested mosquitos and flesh eating bacteria... I was nervous but felt a little better that Tasha would be sober our first night.

As we walked into the ceremonial house called a maloka everyone was quiet and serious. No one spoke or looked at each other. It was so serious and quiet that it was a bit intimidating – everyone seemed nervous like they were about to confront their inner demons. My nervousness and excitement kept growing. They called us up one by one to drink the tea – it was thick like honey and super sweet with a taste of molasses, coffee, chocolate, battery acid and vomit all rolled into one flavor... It felt like a hot liquid fire in my stomach and I was instantly nauseated.

I had only drank a small amount this first night so I didn't have a huge intense experience. No insights or revelations but I did have just one vision – a snake women came and smiled to me and gave me a welcoming and friendly caress – a sort of hello. I took it as a good sign, but little did I know what I would be in for the next couple ceremonies. One thing that struck me and impressed me this first night though was the sound of the shaman's medicine songs. They call these songs icaros and the songs are a fundamental aspect of any Ayahuasca ceremony. The icaros are considered to be plant medicine coming through the mouths of the shamans – the shamans let the plants sing through them in a way and this is a form of energy work that guides the visions of the ceremony and cleans out the negative energies. Ricardo was doing things with his voice I never knew was possible before – he had a deep and loud vibratory resonance in his songs that I could feel in my body. Just listening to him sing I thought to myself – this is the first real magician I have ever seen. This is the first person I have ever seen perform real magic. I had been in 2 mystery schools and studied with a number of other teachers who all claimed to practice magic or healing – but this was a whole different level. I was excited to see what would happen the next night when I drank more of the medicine.

The second night I was still a bit nervous and everyone entered the maloka for ceremony looking super serious and quiet again. Sitting in a grass roof hut in the middle of the jungle in the dark getting ready to drink a powerful hallucinogen can be intimidating. I drank more this night. It was maybe the worst nightmare of my life.

The medicine kicked in real quick and real strong for me. I was instantly super sick and in every kind of pain imaginable. I was nauseous, had muscle aches and cramps, had a fever with hot and cold flashes, started sweating and had intense pressures in my head. Everything hurt more than I had ever felt anything hurt in my life. I was very scared. The shamans hadn't even started singing yet – I was silently begging for them to start soon. I was begging for the night to be over – begging to go back and not drink the Ayahuasca. It felt as if my soul was being ripped out of me – I had a very real seeming fear that these shamans would steal my soul and leave me empty and brainwashed. I started puking like crazy – violent painful puking that cramped and hurt my whole body. The Ayahuasca tasted horrible when I had drunk it but it was a thousand times worse coming up. I wanted to beg for help, but it was too late – I had already drunk the Ayahuasca and there was no going back. I didn't know what to do – I had never felt so powerless and weak in my life.

A couple minutes into my loud violent retching Ricardo started to sing. Suddenly 3 voices were singing. It felt like his song was pulling more puke from my body. The song was doing things I had never experienced or dreamed of before – it filled my body and vibrated throughout my soul. I kept puking and couldn't stop. I can still remember the enchanted sound of these three voices singing – all singing their own songs and creating and intricate web of harmonies and disharmonies that only the Shipibo can produce. I thought all three voices were coming out of Ricardo at first and was baffled – it took me hours to realize that a second shaman named Wiler had joined this ceremony and the third voice was an apprentice named Felipe.

After hours of puking and extreme pain and horror the medicine slowly started to wear off a little bit. I had zero insights or visions the whole night – just pain. I went to sleep still sick and very scared and confused.

The next day when I woke up I felt horrible. I was still super sick from the night before and very weak. I was totally confused what was going on and I wanted more than anything to flee the center and never come back. But I had spent years dreaming about trying Ayahuasca and it was hard to let that go. I didn't understand why my ceremony had been so difficult and I didn't see any benefits from it – I came feeling happy and healthy but now I just felt weak and sick. I thought this was supposed to be medicine? I had heard it could be hard, but I thought the pain might make more sense if it felt like I was healing something or processing some trauma. Instead all I had was suffering and pain with no conscious reason why.

I asked the doctor Joe about the experience and he told me to just stick with it and trust the process. We had a night off before our third ceremony – I still felt sick even after another day of rest, but I showed up ready to drink.

The third ceremony was a repeat of the second one. Incredible pain with no visions or insights or explanation why. I wanted to leave even more then I had after the previous ceremony. I thought back to San Pedro and how wonderful ceremony with Lesley had been – deep insights, connection and healing, and no suffering. Some challenges sure, but they all made sense and I could see the benefits right away. I wished dearly I could be back with her and San Pedro.

I thought about asking them to drive us back to Iquitos and getting out of there... But then I thought of all the years wondering about Ayahuasca and feeling Ayahuasca call me. I thought of how little money we had and how it had taken 6 years for me to save up just for the first trip to Peru. I didn't think it was likely that I would find myself back in Peru anytime soon with how hard it had been the first time. We had signed up for 2 weeks of dieting including 7 Ayahuasca ceremonies and I somehow knew that if I didn't see it through I would regret it. I would get home and wonder what would have happened if I had stayed. Would the medicine have opened up for me and taught me something wonderful? Would I miss out on something and always regret it? I knew that I would regret not seeing it through and always have questions and doubts if I left early – and at the same time felt that if I gave Ayahuasca the benefit of the doubt and a fair chance over two weeks that I would be able to leave knowing I had seen it through and given it the full opportunity to show itself.

I talked to Joe that day and he asked me to describe my childhood. He said the shamans didn't really know what to help me with since I had told them everything was fine. He wanted to know if I had had any past trauma or anything like that. I told him that my mother had committed suicide and that had been very traumatic, but I also felt that I had healed it over the last few years and had already done a bit of work in that area. He thought it was a good place for the shamans to start working and likely there was more there to work on still.

I was very frustrated and scared walking into ceremony the 4th night. Tasha had had wonderful insights and healing in her ceremonies, but I had only trouble. I thought maybe this wasn't the plant for me. I loved the songs they were singing and the raw display of real magic and power... But I hated the suffering that just left me feeling sick and weak afterward. The ceremony started the same as normal – I felt the nausea coming back and thought to myself "Oh no, another repeat!" But something shifted. I don't know where the impulse or idea came from, but instead of resisting my puke I embraced it and welcomed it and started dancing over my bucket like a snake. I swayed back and forth looking into the bucket and waiting for the puke to come. I had the gentlest most pleasant puke ever, and as my vomit landed in my bucket my spirit simultaneously left my body. I became pure energy and light and was One with everything. I saw the true nature of my spirit and saw the truth of death. I felt the deep peace that only death can bring – just like when I had been drowning in the ocean. I saw all of creation and I understood then how death was the greatest healer.

Ayahuasca showed me how much she loved us humans and how she wanted to help us. She showed me how her love can be a tough love – like a surgeon causing you great pain to cut you open while saving your life. She showed me how she wanted to help us humans before we destroy ourselves. As we poison the planet and destroy the rain forests and each other with industrialization and war we forget our true nature. We forget that we are all connected and that we all share this planet together. Harming the planet and harming each other only invites more sickness into our own lives. She showed me how she was trying to educate us and help us find love for each other so we could save ourselves. She also showed me that if we don't save ourselves the planet will kill us all before we kill her completely. Plants and animals will live on. And in death we will be healed – as we die we remember who we are and find connection to the infinite and the deep peace that only death can bring. I was hard for me to come back to my body and leave that peace. Death heals all, but I wasn't truly dead yet – I was only getting a preview.

I came back to my body and was in extreme bliss. I could barely keep from jumping up and down and screaming with joy. I bounced silently on my mat shaking my hands in gratitude towards the sky. I realized that as I had fallen in love with Tasha I had learned to fear death again – I was afraid she would die and leave me, or that I would die and leave her with that pain of loss. Ayahuasca was reminding me of a lesson that almost drowning and that the mushrooms had taught me years before – there is no need to fear death.

We had 3 more ceremonies after that – all good. Some were gentler and more subtle, and one in particular for me was very powerful and insightful. Tasha did a lot of personal work and actually healed her chronic back pain. For 3 years her back pain would get so intense sometimes that she couldn't leave the house and it held her back so much. She had seen all kinds of bodywork specialists and done all kinds of treatments at home but nothing worked. But after our first visit to Peru and a few ceremonies with San Pedro and Ayahuasca she learned that repressed emotions and trauma were causing her back pain. As she processed and healed those traumas her back pain left and years later it has still not returned. As challenging as it was, our first Ayahuasca retreat was very good for us.

Back Home – Integrating Ceremonies

By the time Tasha and I left Nihue Rao we had gotten a pretty good impression of the Ayahuasca tradition, and we absolutely loved everything about San Pedro and the Cusco area. We had been traveling and doing medicine work for about 6 weeks and had left the last 2 weeks of our stay in Peru as a time to integrate all the medicine work before returning home as well as a time to get off the beaten path and see more of Peru. We both came to Peru wondering if it would be a place we might want to move to sometime in the future, so we were really excited to explore more.

We had flown into Iquitos, but to save money and have a little more adventure we left the city on a cargo boat. We were packed in with hundreds of people into hammocks on the deck of a boat with a bunch of cargo getting transported upstream. This was great as we were traveling with mostly locals and really had a lot of time to sit and think about all our recent ceremonies while we watched the river float by. The boat took us to Yuramaguas and from there we took buses and taxis to Tarapoto and all the way up to Chachapoyas. Near Chachapoyas we visited a wonderful waterfall and also some ancient ruins called Kuelap. From there we bused to Chaclayo to visit the ruins of Sipan as well as a rare local desert forest reserve. Then we bused further south to Trujillo to visit the Moche and Chan Chan ruins. Each temple or city of ruins we visited was completely different and all based on the local nature – we really appreciated the beauty and energy of everywhere we visited. This part of the trip wasn't focused on medicine but we used this time as a sort of integration period before returning back home to the states.

When we eventually got home we only had 3 days before flying to Hawaii to vacation with Tasha's family. She has some younger siblings and her parents put us up in the Disney Land Resort there. This was a real hard transition after Peru. We went from staying places with no electricity and spending time with people who had no money or running water to staying at a resort where they spoil kids left and right and everything costs loads of money. In Peru we watched little kids always being well behaved and often having the time of their lives digging up potatoes with their mother or playing with an empty coke bottle in the dirt. In Hawaii there were kids with water slides and candy and video games screaming at their parents and acting like life was horrible... It was a very sharp contrast, and after becoming so settled into the culture and lifestyle of Peru it was hard to understand and relate to being back in the USA.

We went from Hawaii to Utah to visit my family and then when we got home we visited the redwoods for our second time ever – the redwoods were beautiful and seemed like a little taste of peace and paradise in the USA. We camped out in nature the whole time and went to visit our favorite tree again of course. By the time we got home we had spent every penny we had but luckily we found work again very quickly, and while things were tough for a while it all worked out perfectly in the end. Being broke for a month when we got home was totally worth all the traveling.

Integrating into being back home was hard though. In Peru we felt connected to this culture who really respected and revered plant medicines and nature. People had strong family values and didn't need money to be happy. Back at home everyone was so busy all the time and everything revolved around money and work. Everyone seemed depressed or anxious in the USA and people were just less connected wherever we went. We had gotten use to the support of our plant medicine allies and community, and now back at home we felt like all our allies and community were in Peru – it felt a little lonely.

For a while we didn't go back to doing our own ceremonies with plants – we thought we could use a break after having done so many ceremonies in Peru. We really wanted to integrate the work we had already done. After about a month or longer we started thinking a ceremony back at home might help us integrate back into the USA and get a little more grounded in our home. I had recently been reading about Amanita Muscaria mushrooms which I had never felt called to before and the experiences a few friends told me about made me think I should look into them. Within a few days of hearing their experiences and thinking I should connect with this mushroom I saw one for the first time in my life

– it was growing on the lawn of a Buddhist temple in Seattle and I picked and prepared it.

We went to a local park that has tons of beautiful woods and beach. We consumed the mushrooms and had a nice and gentle ceremony at the park. As we got back to the house we decided to go for another short night time walk and ended up at another empty park with a merry go round. I laid back on the merry go round and looked up into the sky as I was slowly rotating around – suddenly the sky turned into a vortex and I was sucked inside. I saw my dead mother and I started crying. I realized how much grief I still had around losing my mother and in that moment I saw what the shamans had been doing for me in the jungle. While they had sung to me about my mother for 7 ceremonies in a row, I hadn't had a single insight or vision of my mother in ceremony. I asked Ayahuasca about her but got nothing. It had taken that many ceremonies to break down the walls I had around my grief. Now that those walls were gone it was the Amanita that took me into the grief so I could experience and get to know it a bit. I also saw a book – this book was about healing and magic and the Amanita said it was my family's book of healing and that I could access it when I was ready.

Since coming back home from Peru I was wondering where my path was. I knew I wanted to work with plant medicines but I didn't know which one I wanted to focus on. I didn't know if it was better for me to focus on one plant medicine or on a few different ones – the Amanitas told me that I was a Jack-of-all-Trades medicine worker and that my path would involve many plants. The Amanita showed me how these plants could work together through me and taught me that I didn't need to separate these plants into separate traditions, but that I just needed to focus on their healing potential and learn when to work with which ones.

The Amanita also told me that next time I worked with it I should ask it to teach me about death and abandonment. So Tasha and I went to another park to scope it out planning to do an Amanita ceremony there the very next day. As we scoped the park out it was normal, but the next day when we showed up to do ceremony around death and abandonment there was suddenly hundreds of dead salmon all over the park with their eyes poked out and their guts and eggs spilled all over the park. Returning to the park many years in a row I never saw anything like it ever again – it was only the one time that the park was covered in dead salmon. This quickly became a theme with our Amanita ceremonies – synchronicities in the world around us that timed themselves perfectly to the ceremony we were in.

Our First Home Diet

Dieting in Peru can be expensive. Not only is the plane ticket expensive, but staying at a retreat center is expensive as well. We didn't know when we would be able to afford to return to Peru and we wanted to see if dieting on our own could be as effective as dieting under a teacher. We decided to diet without using Ayahuasca for the first round and settled on a local plant called stinging nettle. We chose stinging nettle because it was so readily available and easy to forage where we live and out intuition guided us to begin with this plant. We went into the forest and when we found a good patch we prayed and asked if we could use its leaves for medicine. We blew mapacho (jungle tobacco) smoke on the leaves and then gathered some and left a rolled mapacho for the plants as an offering. We didn't restrict our diet quite as much as we had at Nihue Rao but we decided to go with no sex, no oils, no salt, no heavier meats, no spices and no sugar. We dieted the leaves of stinging nettle 3 times for a week each time (3 weeks total).

Around this time I had also become curious to check out another plant called Salvia Divinorum. I had smoked this plant years before but I wanted to connect with it in the traditional way this time – by chewing the leaves. So I ordered a large bag of dried leaves and did a couple ceremonies with Tasha. We were very impressed with Salvia. When you smoke the plant it causes very intense and uncomfortable visions that are difficult to understand, but when you chew it you enter this very comfortable and gentle experience where you can talk directly to the spirit of the plant. Afterwards we sometimes noticed we were having prophetic dreams that would come true a few days later – it was like Salvia was showing off to us a bit. At one point I even sang my first icaro during a Salvia trance – my voice changed into something I had never heard before and couldn't replicate afterwards and I channeled a song in a language I didn't know, but which sounded similar to medicine songs I had heard in Peru. The song made my whole body vibrate and I felt great and energized afterwards. I was blown away and excited and wondered how to repeat the experience – because I had no clue how to do it again.

One day I decided to ask Salvia to help me heal grief around my mother's suicide. With Salvia you have to meet the plant half-way and it is very important to sit very still and very quiet in a dark room. Her spirit is skittish like a deer and she doesn't like fast movement, loud sounds or bright lights. So I was going into my meditation and suddenly Salvia appears. She tells me, "There is a spliff with some cannabis on your dresser – go smoke it." I was confused as this would interrupt my ceremony and I was trying to connect with Salvia, but I went along with the instructions. I smoked the spliff and then laid back down. Immediately the spirit of cannabis appeared to me for the first time in my life.

Cannabis told me "Everything is fine with us, but you shouldn't smoke me for the next 7 days." I said that was fine and then she went away. Salvia came back and replaced cannabis to give me further instructions. She told me to diet the root of stinging nettle instead of the leaves and said it would help me heal my grief. She told me to start the diet the next day and continue for 7 days and also said that I could use Salvia for ceremony during any of those days as well if I wanted to go deeper into the diet. I decided since Salvia said I could use her during the nettle root diet that I would just diet both plants at the same time.

I had heard of Ayahuasca teaching people about other plants and helping people go deeper during diets – it is supposed to be her specialty. I had never heard about anything like that with Salvia, but this diet was powerful and very deep. Salvia really helped me connect with nettle root in a big way, and the previous 3 weeks of dieting nettle leaves finally came together and I made a deep connection with this plant.

Three days into my diet I was reading another book about San Pedro and about Lesley. In the book Lesley was talking about how her father had died, and when he did he started appearing to her in visions during ceremony and became one of your closest spirit guides. Suddenly I started bawling and couldn't stop. I was overwhelmed with emotion out of nowhere. I was sober sitting in a chair but I suddenly had a vivid vision where my mother appeared to me and taught me about her suicide. She told me that she had chosen to be born into a life that would push her to suicide and I had chosen a life that I would lose my mother –

and that the relationship we had together allowed a special connection that we could only have through that loss. She told me her suicide had a deeper purpose and that she would always be with me.

The next night I drank Salvia tea before bed to have a journey that would turn into dream space and sleep. This can be a powerful time to work with Salvia. I had visions as the plant opened my energy and I soon saw nettle root – the root looked like a giant finger and started digging deep inside my body cleaning me out. It pulled all this old nasty energy out of my body and I could feel lighter and lighter the more it took. When it finished cleaning me I then left my body and went into old memories. I saw myself as a child and saw that I was very scared and alone. I suddenly remembered when this had happened – it was a memory I had totally forgotten. In the vision I was able to protect myself and comfort the child in that memory – a type of soul retrieval that Salvia and nettle were guiding me through together. As I comforted this part of me that was scared and traumatized, it entered back into my body and found peace.

The Salvia visions continued and next took me to a vision of my mother as a child. She was in a bad situation and someone was going to hurt her – I had the feeling this was an event that had started her depression in some ways. In the vision I was able to stop the person from hurting her and protect her – in a way this was another soul retrieval, but for my mother. I had the feeling I was helping her spirit heal something that was also having a trickle down healing effect for myself. The vision eventually turned into sleep where I was comforted by the Salvia spirit in my dreams.

When I finished this diet I had the insight that while it is a little easier dieting isolated in the jungle, it was still possible to go very deep into the dieta experience on my own at home as well.

Vegetalismo – Spiritual Herbalism

Vegetalismo is the Amazonian name for the practice of dieting plants. This is a form of spiritual herbalism where you can connect directly with the spirit of a plant for healing and learning. In the Ayahuasca tradition advanced dieting is a form of apprenticeship. In this practice, you restrict your diet and your lifestyle to create the most welcoming environment for the plants spirit to enter your being. You are also taking away stimulus to make yourself more sensitive to the subtle influence of the plants spirit and at the same time making a gesture of dedication and discipline to the plant through sacrifice. A common Amazonian dieta might be plain fish with either plain rice or potato and some green plantains – nothing else. During this period, you connect with your chosen plant each day – often through drinking it as a tea or juice, but sometimes just by smelling it or bathing in infused water, or some other way. Connecting with the plant while on this restricted diet allows the plants spirit stronger influence over your body, and allows the plant to metaphorically grow inside of you. By inviting this plant in, you allow yourself to benefit from its wisdom and healing power.

Usually this type of plant dieta is kept from any time between a week to 3 months per plant. Sometimes as long as a year can be spent with just one plant. For healing purposes, anywhere from a week to a month is common, and apprentices may diet their plant longer in an attempt to form an alliance with that plants spirit for future work. Most often, these plants are not psychedelic in any way, but the restricted diet which can be similar to a fast works in a way to let you hear these plants speak to you and heal you. You can do this practice with almost any plant in the world, though the most common plants are Amazonian since this is where the practice originates. Common plants from the Amazon include; Oje, Ajo Sacha, Chiric Sanango, Chuchuwasha, Mucura, Ortega, Lupuna tree's, Mapacho, Ayahuma, Bobinsana and many others. Some plants will help you have more vivid diets because they have more spiritual force – these are called "master plants" and usually are the only plants people really diet.

There is no reason this practice needs to be restricted to the Amazon though. This practice works great with plants anywhere, and more recently, some students of Amazonian vegetalismo have begun working with plants native to their own homes in Europe and North America. Oak, Acacia, Cedar, Sage, Cacao, Tulsi, Nettle, Blackberry, and Devils Club are all great plants to diet at home. I have even heard of other indigenous cultures using similar techniques to dieta, without contact to the Amazon – for example, I met an Australian who dieted Strangler Fig as part of a traditional Aboriginal apprenticeship! This technique probably resembles practices from many regions and cultures. Because my personal experience is with learning this practice from the Amazon, and localizing it to my home in North America, I will talk mostly about working with plants from those regions and perspectives.

When the apprentice performs dieta, they usually want something more than just personal healing – they want to learn from the plant how they can help others heal as well. Usually the diet begins and ends with an Ayahuasca ceremony. Since Ayahuasca is the "mother of all plants," she can teach you greatly about the plant you are dieting (this is considered one of her most important roles in the Amazon). By restricting your diet, you also make your body weak, so that the plants spirit can influence you more easily. You metaphorically become "like a plant" so that the spirit can comfortably grow within your body. If you successfully complete your diet, the plant has accepted you, and will be your spirit ally from then on – you can call on them any time, because they are always with you. When Ayahuasquero's perform healing and sing icaros, they are often singing the song of a plant they dieted in the past to call on that plants spirit for healing the client. There song can even provide the same effect as physically taking the plant. The greatest sign of success with a diet is if the plant teaches you its song.

This diet can often be strict – common diets often include potatoes, rice, or some form of yucca, and green (unripe) plantains. Usually you also get a little fish. For longer diets, or specific plants, the diet might even include days of fasting completely. This is a sort of trial which the apprentice must pass if they want to prove their dedication to the plant and open their body to its spirit. During the diet, the plant will often test and tempt them, and the apprentice must learn how to overcome this if they want to work with the spirits for the benefit of others.

Even though all forms of dieta usually show similarities, there are also differences. How long an apprentice diets a plant, or how often they perform dieta may depend on many individual circumstances, including when they have time available, and when they can afford to pay their teacher for services. While some apprentices have no teacher and learn only from the spirits, most do have a teacher who they either work for or pay in exchange for teaching. Some people focus on dieting all kinds of plants, as they want many allies to help them – they might diet plants for only a week (often followed by a week of "post dieting"). Post dieting is a period after you finish your dieta, where you keep some of the dietary restrictions as you slowly re-introduce foods back to your body (during this time, you are not drinking your plant anymore – just keeping some food restrictions and still abstaining from sex).

Another style of dieting focuses on just a few plants, but the apprentice gets to know those allies incredibly deeply. Often the apprentice would diet plants for up to 3 months each or even as long as a year. They might diet for 6-12 months at a time using this style. I have heard of this style of dieting going on as long as 3 straight years for incredibly intense apprenticeships. Some cultures in the Amazon often include apprentices setting aside 2-3 years at the beginning of their training to do an extreme dieta alone in the jungle with just their teacher to check up on them and bring them food. They often say that if you make it through the 2+ years, that you will finish your diet as a shaman and healer, but if you end your diet early, you will emerge a jealous sorcerer who uses their power to harm people (this could be superstition, though I think there is at least a little truth to it). I even know of one healer, who had no teacher, but went by himself into the jungle to diet for 2 years – no one brought him food, and he had no teacher besides the spirits. He is regarded as one of the most effective and well-known healers in the Amazon (the spirits must have protected him in order for him to survive such a quest).

Even for the students who break their diets up and do them more spaced out (most do this), 1-2 years is often considered the minimum amount of time spent dieting to become an effective healer. Many learn some healing skills before this long, but around 2+ years seems to be the ideal time (some people even do up to 8 years straight). Usually 2 years dieting takes many more years to accumulate though (if you dieting 3 months a year, it would take 8 years to reach 2 years of dieting), and even after so much dieting, it takes many years of helping all kinds of clients in all types of situations before you are an expert. The most sought after shamans are the ones with 25+ years of experience.

Another commonly held belief associated with dieta is that breaking the diet early can sometimes be harmful. This is considered a quick way to offend the spirit of the plant. Sick clients who don't finish their diet sometimes become more sick, and apprentices who do not finish diets correctly may become brujos (negative connotation for a sorcerer who harms others) or may become sick, lose their power, or die (I haven't heard of anyone dying, but I have heard the claim that it is possible). Specific plants are considered especially dangerous to fail your diet with – mostly the more powerful allies like great hardwood trees (lapuna, oak ect), mapacho, or toé/datura.

You do not have to limit dieting to plants either – traditionally some people will also diet stones. I have even met a few rare people who dieted mushrooms. Since you wouldn't eat or drink a stone the way this is done is by transferring the stones vibration/energy to some water and drinking the water. You put a stone in a cup of water over night – usually left outside in the moon and starlight. In the morning you take out the stone and drink the water with your intention to connect with the essence of the stone. You would follow similar dietary restrictions and methods as dieting a plant.

To make dieting at home easier for you I have included a couple sample dietary procedures which I have learned from different practitioners. Each of these styles is unique. You can try any of these styles or try to modify and create your own style if you like. My biggest suggestion is that if you make a commitment to a plant that you see it through and stay on course to what you agreed to.

Traditional Diet with Ayahuasca and a Master Plant:

Some version of this style dieta is what is most commonly practiced in the Amazon. If you go to diet at an Ayahuasca center you will most likely diet similar to this, and sometimes they will have you start a pre-dieta diet before you arrive. First day of your diet you might begin with a purgative of some kind to clean you out. The shaman will also select a plant for you to diet based on what healing you need and you will agree on a certain amount of time to keep the diet. That night you will sit in ceremony with Ayahuasca and the shaman will sing a song to you to open your diet.

The next day you will start drinking your plant each afternoon. Usually you either drink a tea or you drink the leaves of the plant blended with a little water into a type of juice. When you drink your plant you always pray to it first and either blow the prayers into the plant or sing a little song to it to create the spiritual connection. Each day you will spend your time in isolation thinking about and trying to connect to your plant. You often will also avoid media of this kind – limited or no reading, listening to music or watching TV, and usually limited contact with others. Time is spent meditating, praying, or maybe writing and making art.

You will eat the same exact foods every day. An example diet might be plain oatmeal with a green banana for breakfast and then bony river fish and another green banana for lunch. You may also get plain rice or potato with your lunch. Sometimes there is no dinner, or sometimes you get another copy of your lunch meal with dinner. This gets very monotonous but that is part of your sacrifice to the plant.

The diet is then ended with another Ayahuasca ceremony where the shaman will sing to you again to close your diet. The next morning you may eat a little salt with your breakfast and maybe some fruit you haven't been allowed to have in a while. Often times the only Ayahuasca ceremonies are at the start and end of your diet, but sometimes you may have more ceremonies in between as well – it usually depends on how long and advanced your dieta is. Usually the longer a dieta is the less Ayahuasca you drink. Once the diet is finished you usually stay on the Ayahuasca diet for another couple weeks or even months if you finished a longer diet. If you were dieting a plant for 10 days you might actually be pre-dieting for 7 days, doing 10 days of strict dieta with the plant, and then doing 20-30 days post dieta where you slowly reintroduce foods a little at a time. This style of dieta may be performed anywhere from 7 days to a year or longer.

Dieting Without Ayahuasca:

This is an example of a diet which may be easier for some people to perform on their own at home. First choose which plant you will diet and go find this plant in nature. If it is a tree use the outer bark to make a tea and if it is a smaller plant use the leaves to make a type of juice with water in a blender. Sopla the plant or tree (sopla involves blowing tobacco smoke or Agua de Florida from your mouth to bless something). Keep an attitude of gratitude as you collect part of the plant to use in your dieta – if you like you can sing to the plant as well.

Prepare your plant for drinking by first soplaing any tools you will use to make the drink in. With tree bark make tea by sitting the bark in water for a few hours and with other plants blend the leaves as mentioned. Once finished also sopla the mixture. When you are ready to enter the diet sing into your drink and pray with it – then drink it down! You are now in your diet. Repeat this step each day of your diet – try to drink at the same time each day and always with prayers and gratitude.

During the diet avoid heavy meats, pork, oils, salt, sugar, spices, processed foods, dairy, sex, alcohol or drugs and powerful herbs. Good foods include chicken breast, fresh water fish, eggs, legumes, veggies, fruit is okay if it isn't too sweet or sugary, potato and rice. A little coconut oil is okay for cooking if needed and some cilantro, basil or oregano can be okay for flavor (stay away from stronger spices like cumin or pepper ect). Also avoid stimulants, caffeine, and contact with people who might have recently used recreational substances. As much isolation as you can do is better and also avoid media if possible – more time spent focusing on your plant is better. If you really want to take this diet deeper it is also possible to fast for a day or two (keep drinking water though).

Usually this style of dieting is shorter – maybe 5-8 days with the first day being when you first drink the plant. This diet works especially well with trees or with mapacho – I originally learned this diet from someone who focuses on tree diets.

You end this style of diet by taking salt. Use half a teaspoon of nice salt like sea or rock salt. Sing into the salt then swish it around in your mouth for about 30-40 seconds before spitting it out. Then swish water to rinse out the salt and spit that out as well – your diet is now finished.

Along with the 5-8 diet it is good to avoid street or recreational drugs for at least 30 days and avoid sex for 15+ days. Also try to wait a few days before adding back into your diet refined sugar, acidic fruits, cheese or heavy grease. Since these diets are shorter you may find yourself wanting to diet the same plant multiple times to keep deepening your connection.

Microdose Ayahuasca Diet:

This is a style of dieting which I thought up one day which can also be easier to perform at home if you make your own Ayahuasca. It involves cooking your Ayahuasca normally but by adding the plant you want to diet into the Ayahuasca itself during the cooking process. Choose a length of time to diet and also choose how much you will restrict your diet – I suggest going at least without sugar, oils, salt, heavy meats, dairy, fermented foods, sex and media if possible. Focus on fresh veggies and fruit (not too sweet), chicken breast, fish, eggs, legumes and starches like rice or potato.

When you make the Ayahuasca with your chosen plant added to it make lots of prayers and sing to your medicine. When you are ready to start the diet make a declaration to yourself and the plants by stating out loud or in your head your plans and intentions. Then each night before bed take a spoonful of the Ayahuasca you made making sure to pray to the Ayahuasca and to your plant before ingesting it. Try to spend lots of time during the day attempting to talk to your plant and attempting to still your mind and body so you can listen. Try this for 7-14 days straight and when you are finished close your diet with a prayer or song and by adding a little salt to your meal. Keep up your dietary restrictions for 2 weeks afterwards.

Dieting with Salvia Divinorum:

I have only tried this once and feel like more testing would be good before confirming this method works well, but because I shared the story of my personal diet with Salvia I thought I should mention this method here. I would recommend abstaining from sex, oils, heavy meats, salt, sugar, fermented/aged foods and any drugs or alcohol. I would also cut out any strong medicine plants – like certain herbal teas or supplements. This would be a minimum – you can get deeper results by going stricter if you like.

Each day in the morning or afternoon you can drink your chosen plant for dieta. Once a day, or less if you prefer, you can also work with Salvia doing either the quid method or by making a cold pressed tea (method for quidding Salvia or making a cold-pressed tea are in The Plant Remedy book). I recommend ingesting the Salvia at a different time of day then when you work with your other plant – so if you drink your dieta plant in the morning, maybe you would work with Salvia in the evening. Salvia ceremony can often be deepest first thing in the morning or last thing before bed – the sleepy relaxed state when you are close to dream time is very conducive to working with Salvia.

....

With any of these styles of dieting really spend a lot of time trying to focus on connecting to your plant. Don't break the diet early if you can avoid it – make a commitment and stick to it. Also try to avoid lusting after the things you cannot have – dreaming all day of things you are sacrificing for the plant is not only considered rude to the plant, but it makes you diet harder for yourself as well. You may notice the plant talking to you in dreams, in your head, in Ayahuasca ceremony, or you may not hear much – sometimes the plant starts talking to you more in the weeks following your diet then during the actual diet itself. It is also common for the first few diets to be more subtle and for you to have more noticeable communication with the plant as you get more experienced – so don't get discouraged if it takes a few tries to really connect with the plants and have a deeper diet. If you stick with this practice you will see the rewards. Dieta is incredibly powerful – maybe the most powerful plant medicine practice of all.

Married in Peru

"The best thing to hold onto in life is each other." ~ Audrey Hepburn

Tasha and I had been working with the plants at home and making a lot of progress, but we both felt like we had some unfinished business in Peru. We still wondered if we might want to move there sometime and we both felt like there was a lot more we could learn from the traditions there. We were searching for some way to solidify the connections we had made with people on our last trip and also for a way to spend more time there on a limited budget.

Tasha and I had also told our families we were engaged and were trying to figure out what kind of wedding we wanted. When we had been in Peru Lesley's son Simon had told us how sometimes they would host wedding ceremonies at the Condor Temple outside their house – we had almost asked them to perform a ceremony for us right then and there but felt like our families might be sad to miss our wedding... So we tried to think of a fun way to join our families closer to home, but all the ideas we thought of didn't really seem like they were for us – all our ideas seemed more geared to pleasing our friends or families. So we kept talking about it but not really getting any clear ideas that felt right.

One night we were talking about this with my parents and they said, "Actually, we are kinda surprised you guys don't want to get married in Peru or something."

"Well, would you guys come to Peru if we were getting married there? We don't want anyone to feel left out..."

"Of course! We want you guys to have the perfect wedding for you. We will come to your wedding no matter where it is."

Tasha and I went for a short walk after dinner and talked for about 5 minutes before we realized that we knew exactly where we wanted to get married and exactly who we wanted to marry us. We checked with Tasha's parents and they were supportive of the travel idea too.

When we had met Lesley in Peru we were both incredibly touched by her personality and her medicine and her home and garden – we loved everything about her. More than anyone we knew she embodied deep passionate and compassionate love and we thought the energy of her personality and her home would be the perfect way to start our marriage together. I emailed her to see if she would perform the ceremony – she was so excited! She felt flattered that we thought so highly of her after our short visit and so special that we asked her to marry us – no one had ever asked her to marry them before and we somehow instantly became closer to her through asking her for this. I think this really kickstarted our friendship with her. When Simon had told me people would get married at The Condor Temple he had meant that people wanted to be married by the exotic local indigenous shamans like the Q'ero tribe or another famous shaman named Puma – we thought he was talking about Lesley marrying people, and had no clue we were the first ones to have that idea.

We didn't really plan many of the wedding details but we did pick a date during a full moon and I started to plan a retreat for our families. Tasha and I didn't really have enough money for another Peru trip, but by planning our wedding in Peru we actually got a group discount for bringing our families that made the trip much more affordable, and Lesley was kind to gift us some free time to stay at her house. Our families paid for our wedding so this trip ended up being much less expensive than it would have otherwise. Somehow all the pieces were coming together and it felt like opportunities were dropping straight into our laps. It felt as if the whole universe was conspiring to help us.

I planned a 7 day trip for our families to join us on – we took them to Ollantaytambo, Pisac and Machu Picchu, and we showed them around Cusco. I had been toying with the idea of trying to host retreats in Peru at Lesley's house, and this seemed like the perfect test run to see if I could do it. After some sightseeing we had the wedding planned at Lesley's house, and then our families would head back home and Tasha and I would stay longer to do more ceremonies and traveling. We wanted to make the most of this trip again so we decided to quit our jobs a second time and travel for 2 months in Peru.

We told our friends and family that they were all welcome to come to the wedding, but that we figured it would be a smaller group since travel is so expensive. 12 people decided to join us, 10 family members and 2 friends, but at the last second one friend dropped out. His name was Steve (name changed for privacy) and he had been planning on doing a bunch of ceremony with us and was hoping for healing as he was in a real dark place and feeling suicidal. He called me 3 days before the trip and said "I'm sorry, I can't go. I'm not ready to be happy yet. Have a beautiful wedding." I was shocked and a bit heartbroken – a lesson that we all have to be committed to our own healing and that for many a familiar sickness is less scary then an unfamiliar new life of joy.

Tasha and I got down to Peru a week before the rest of the family. We wanted to get settled in, plan the wedding details and also drink San Pedro with Lesley and reconnect with the plants. That ceremony we asked San Pedro to teach us how to be good partners for each other and to help us have a happy and loving marriage together – I cannot think of any better blessing for a newlywed couple. There was also a special surprise waiting for us at Lesley's – a Q'ero shaman named Louis Q'espe was there to share some of his healing expertise. We had read about the Q'ero tribe and also heard about them from people we met on our last visit to Peru – they are thought by many to be the most traditional and most gifted healers in the Andes. I even had a book about the Q'ero with me called "Masters of the Living Energy" that I was reading. Tasha and I were blown away because we had been reading about them and wanting to meet them for 2 years – and we didn't even have to find them because one found us!

San Pedro was more powerful than I had remembered. Maybe Lesley had started to make her brew stronger, or maybe I was just more ready for the downloads, but I had a hugely transformative ceremony. I started singing icaros again – some sounded like Quechua and I recognized some as Hebrew. I know neither language but somehow I was singing songs completely in those languages which I had never heard before. I couldn't stop shaking and singing as floods of energy were pouring into my body.

Then San Pedro said something interesting to me, "How come you didn't pour me for anyone?"

I suddenly remembered the year before when I thought San Pedro had told me to share his medicine back at home. I had assumed it was just my ego talking and had dismissed it…. I still thought it must be my ego, but I humored myself a little and said, "Are you sure? Well I guess I could give it a try…" I mentally told the voice I thought was San Pedro that I would share the medicine when I got home, but at the same time I was still thinking to myself "No way am I ready for that… I would love to apprentice though… Maybe one day I will be ready."

We had a great ceremony and learned a lot about each other – San Pedro had given us both a lot of practical advice on how to be supportive and understanding of each other. Tasha and I share many similar interests, but in many other ways we have really different personalities so this advice was very helpful. We also received a cleansing from the Q'ero shaman Louis, and afterwards we saw he had some of his tribes healing tools which were available for sale – Tasha and I both bought an altar cloth called a mestana and each got a set of 7 chunpi kuya stones – magic stones shaped by Louis himself that are used for doing energy work. These were powerful medicine tools used for thousands of years by the Andean people and immediately these became our personal altars and we were closely tied to them. Louis was even kind enough to give Lesley, Tasha and me a private workshop on how to work with the altar and stones according to his traditions. These items didn't leave our sides the rest of our journey and we took them to Machu Picchu and every other temple we visited – we didn't mind carrying a big bundle of rocks and crystals because we were so in love with our new altars.

The next day we sat down with Lesley to plan the wedding as well as ask about some different activities we were hoping to do while in the Cusco area. We told her while we were in Peru we really hoped to do a despatcho offering with the Q'ero tribe. Despatcho is a special offering made to the earth, the sun and the mountain spirits asking for their blessings, and these offerings are the main ceremony performed by the Q'ero tribe when in need of healing, abundance or anything else they want help from the spirits with. Lesley asked if we wanted that to be part of the wedding and that sounded perfect! After about 15 minutes talking with Lesley we had the whole wedding planned out and she took care of everything for us – it was the easiest wedding planning ever, but had everything we wanted and looked perfect.

Our families arrived and we took them to all the Sacred Valley temples. Our families weren't ready to try any plant medicines yet, but something special happened to them just from visiting the temples. I remember we had that awesome guide Miguel again and in one of the temples he recommended we close our eyes and have a moment of silence. Afterwards my uncle pulled me aside and said "Did you feel that? Something happened at that temple – I felt something like a spirit – what was that?" Even without ingesting the plants our families were touched by the magic of Peru. The culture and the land rubbed off on them and everyone returned home different. Lighter and happier – maybe even more in love.

We had no intention of pushing any plant medicines on our families – Tasha and I both believe that it is something a person must be drawn to and decide to do on their own, and that it is best to not convince people into it. But our families talked to the locals and saw San Pedro cactus's growing in peoples gardens. They saw the temples and the plant inspired artwork. They all quickly became curious about San Pedro and kept asking us questions. I think if there had been a free day at the end of our retreat that many of them would have been open to drinking. We were just happy that they seemed so open and curious about it though – it certainly changed the way they looked at us and our lifestyle.

The wedding was perfect and beautiful. Louis's brother Juan made a despatcho offering for us and our whole families participated and blew prayers into the coca leaves that were part of the offering.   The coca leaves and the offering became a symbol of our families care and love for us. Juan told us he was putting prayers in for us to start find a new house, a new car, abundant prosperity and many other prayers – they all came true later that year. Tasha was beautiful in her wedding dress and I surprised her with a song I had written in secret months earlier (because we are inseparable she was amazed I found time to write and practice it without her knowing!).

After the despatcho we were surprised when Juan went up to Tasha and threw a cape over her shoulders and then put a hat on her head! Then he came over to me and dressed me in a colorful poncho and Q'ero knitted hat! Lesley laughed, "Oh, I forgot they like to do this! They really like to dress people in their traditional wedding clothes!" We all laughed so hard and Tasha and I got married dressed in the beautiful colorful Q'ero clothing – it was perfect and brought so much laughter to the ceremony.

We walked out of the garden to the Condor Temple right next to Temple of the Moon and they had 3 hearts on the ground made from rose petals waiting for us. We started in the two little hearts on the outside and met in the bigger heart in the middle. Lesley said some beautiful words for us and we shared our vows. We sat in these giant stone thrones carved into the temple – with the wings of the stone condor around us and a stone heart in the center. For thousands of years people have gotten married at this temple and we felt connected to that tradition and blessed to be a part of something so ancient and beautiful.

We took our families to explore the Temple of the Moon and the Frog temple which were both close by – the whole time walking around barefoot. Everything was so perfect. Afterwards we went back to Lesley's garden for cake and champagne and that night we took everyone to our favorite restaurant Pachapapa's where we had the local delicacy cuy (guinea pig). Lesley gifted us a night in the fanciest room of her boutique hotel Andean Wings – it was more than we could ever imagine.

In the morning we were served breakfast and mimosas in bed and later we said adios to the family and continued the rest of our journey on our own.

The Puma With Condor Wings

After the family left we had more ceremonies with Lesley, but the first was the most powerful for me – in fact, it was the most powerful and life changing ceremony I have ever had. Tasha and I were out at dinner with some friends and knew the next day we were going to drink San Pedro. As we left dinner I suddenly became very ill instantly – it felt like something just hit me and I was super sick. I couldn't stop puking and pooping – it was like the worst case of food poisoning ever…. But Tasha and I had shared all our meals that day and she wasn't sick at all – we were totally confused why I was so sick.

We decided to skip ceremony since I was so sick – I just thought it would be a waste since I doubted my ability to hold the medicine down for any length of time. I was sick like this for 5 days and couldn't leave the bedroom at all – so finally I said enough is enough and decided the next morning I would drink San Pedro no matter how horrible I felt. "It's supposed to be medicine right? Well, I am sick, so let's test it out and see if it helps!"

That night I went to sleep knowing that I would drink the next morning no matter how sick I was. I had vivid dreams that night where San Pedro helped me battle demons and bad spirits. San Pedro told me in this dream that I was sick from catching a bad wind in Cusco and started teaching me about the nature of good and evil. A bad wind is harmful energy from somewhere that floats by until it finds a victim – when it comes in contact with them it attacks them and makes them very sick. I had heard about this before but had never experienced it.

The next morning I woke up feeling better than ever. I wasn't sick or weak or tired at all. When I had food poisoning before it had left me weak once I got over it and took me forever to recover from, but this was different – I felt like a million bucks and couldn't wait for ceremony!

A taxi took us up to Lesley's house and as soon as I stepped out of the car I couldn't believe my eyes. Around me were all the other participants getting out of their taxi's…. And a few dozen angels as well! Everywhere I looked there were beings of light that looked just as real and vivid as all the people around me. They were about 8 feet tall and had giant wings, and all of them were singing and shooting light out of their hands and mouths into me. I could hear their song – almost like a high pitched overtone singing, but more perfect and beautiful. They all sang together and kept shooting the light into me – I could feel the light vibrating with their song. It was like seeing a vision of heaven on earth.

I was in awe – this was the most intense, vivid and real vision I had ever had in my life. And I hadn't even drunk the medicine yet. The last mind altering substance I had was San Pedro about 2 weeks before – I was stone cold sober. I knew this was San Pedro but I didn't understand how the ceremony had started before I even drank the medicine. Remembering my dream from the night before I realized that the spirit of San Pedro was really working on me and didn't seem to need me to drink the medicine for it to have a profound effect on my mind and body.

I walked into Lesley's garden and gave her a hug. Louis Q'espe was there again and I shook his hand. I couldn't really talk to them or anyone else though – Lesley's garden was full of angels and they were all still singing. We walked into Lesley's maloka and she started to explain to everyone about San Pedro and the ceremony logistics – but I couldn't listen. All I could do was try and keep it together as the angels kept dazzling me.

Then suddenly 4 spirits walk in through the front door of her maloka – San Pedro came in as a man shaped cactus made of light, my dead mother walked in, and they were followed by the archangel Michael and Jesus. I don't in any way consider myself Christian or believe in the bible, and this was not a Christian or Catholic influenced ceremony so I was very surprised to see the last two. Don't even ask me how I knew it was them – I just knew. As Lesley started to pour the cups of San Pedro for everyone these four spirits each took their place around me in the four corners. Lesley handed me my cup of medicine and as I looked at it I decided I didn't need it – this was already more intense than any cup of medicine I had taken before! I started to hand the cup back to Lesley but Jesus who was behind me put his hands on my back as if to support me while I drank – so I downed it all in one gulp!

I went outside to find a nice quiet place in her garden and the four spirits followed me staying around me in the four corners. All the angels were still singing and these four spirits were singing with them – and all of them were still shooting light into me. I could barely contain myself. The 4 spirits started to rotate and change places around me until Jesus was in the front – he put his hands on my head and started singing straight into my crown. After he finished he looked at me and smiled. I asked him, "So, are you the son of God or something?" and he just replied, "I am just a healer here to help you." I liked that answer. He then started to leave with Michael and I was left with San Pedro and my mother.

I went to sit under a tree and as I leaned against it I could feel the roots of the tree energetically growing up into me from the earth, and I felt the branches start dipping into my head – I felt as if a flower was covering my head like a hat, but the tree had no flowers that I could see – it actually looked kinda dried up. I felt like this flower was over my head and that I was seeing through the flower – my vision was in a gradient that was yellow at the top, then orange, then red at the bottom. My mother stopped singing to look at me and told me that she really liked this tree. I then sat and talked with her and the tree for what seemed like ages. Eventually when our discussion ended I hugged my mother and could feel her physically in my arms even though it was just her spirit. She hugged me back and at that moment she began to grow wings! She wrapped her wings around me so I was in this cocoon, and I felt our energies mixing. I had the intuition that through this ceremony my mother had become an angel and grew these wings, then she said goodbye and flew into the sky. It was the last time I ever saw her.

Right around this time Lesley walked over to me to check in and see how I was doing. I didn't really know what to say, but I asked her what kind of tree I was sitting under. She told me it was Toé. I knew what Toé was – a powerful psychedelic that is also very toxic and related to datura. I would have recognized it if it had any flowers, but since it was the dry season the flowers had fallen off – there was another one across the garden in the shade that still had its flowers – the flowers were yellow at the top, orange in the middle and red at the bottom just like my vision had been. I wondered why my mother liked Toé so much and kept sitting under it. I was rewarded for my curiosity because the plant kept talking to me!

San Pedro and Toé kept trading off teaching me about healing and about me embodying that role in my life. Then San Pedro said he wanted to show me who I am in this life here and now. I started to feel myself transform – I became a giant puma with condor wings! I could see my paws and my wings and I felt strong and powerful. I jumped into the air and started flying.

I flew around Lesley's garden looking down into her neighbor's yards. I flew around Temple of the Moon and further around the city looking at all these other temples I had never seen before. The city of Cusco is surrounded by all kinds of ruins and temples and I went to visit a bunch of them. Somehow the idea came into my head that maybe I could do distance healing while shapeshifted like this and I remembered a friend at home who recently was diagnosed with some digestion problem that was making him bleed when he defecated – I decided to try and do energy work for him as this condor/puma. I saw his spirit before me and I started to eat the bad energies I saw in his intestines.

Eventually I came back to Lesley's garden and felt like myself again – I was no longer the puma with condor wings. At least my shape was human again – I felt like I had seen my inner nature expressed as a vision and in a way I was still that puma. The ceremony continued on for a few more hours, but slowly started to wind down.

The next day Tasha and I went for a hike from Lesley's house – and we actually found many of the temples I had seen from the air in my visions. They were just like what I had seen in ceremony. I also emailed my friend back at home a few days later – he had gone back to the doctor and his illness had healed itself. I hadn't even told him about the energy work I had done before he told me about his check-up. I mentioned it to him after he told me though and we both wondered if the energy work had fixed him up.

The ceremony reminded me of the time Ayahuasca had shown me the nature of my spirit. San Pedro had also shown me my true nature – but as it manifests in this life now. I thought that was interesting how they both showed me different sides of my true nature, and it seemed just like them to pick those areas of my nature to teach me about. Ayahuasca often has that cosmic spiritual focus, and San Pedro is often so practical and grounded in the here and now.

Tasha and I at our favorite redwood tree

Preparing San Pedro cactus to be cooked

Q'ero Paqo Juan Q'espe and our friend Lesley Myburgh making dispatcho offering for us

Wearing Q'ero clothes at our wedding

Enrique and Aimee – Ayahuasca retreat near Pucallpa

Machu Picchu with Juan de Dios Kucho – Shaman of Machu Picchu

We really did carry our mesa's everywhere!

Back to the Jungle and More Travels

After about a month at Lesley's house we went back to the jungle to do another two week dieta and drink more Ayahuasca. We tried a different center this time in Pucallpa called Santuario Huishtin. This center was a little more affordable and more remote and we had heard great things about the maestro Enrique and his wife Aimee. The center was also located on a sacred volcanic river that always had a constant cloud of steam rising off of it which made the whole place look and feel like a mystical hideout from a story book.

We were very impressed with Enrique and Aimee's skill as healers, but pretty early on we realized that it wasn't the time for us to work with more Ayahuasca. We both felt a call to focus on San Pedro more at the moment. One ceremony though I did get a very insightful message – Ayahuasca told me that Tasha was my medicine. It made me think about how insightful and healing deep relationships can be and how lucky I was to have such a powerful and inspiring woman by my side.

When we finished our dieta we went back to Pucallpa for a couple days, and then we went on another traveling adventure off the beaten path. We bused into the mountains from the jungle – first to Tingo Maria, then Huanuco and La Union, and eventually we stopped in Huaraz. Huaraz is amazing and we met a lot of great people there. Right next to Huaraz is a small mountain town called Chavin that we also spent a few days at – a super quiet and tranquil town that also happens to have the world's oldest evidence of San Pedro use in ceremony. Chavin de Huanter is a 3000 year old temple that is part above ground and part underground – it was covered by an avalanche a long time ago and only part of it has been uncovered. Lesley had told us to look for a man named Martin there and suggested we do San Pedro ceremony with him at the temple. She didn't have his contact info but told us to just ask around and we would find him.

Our Spanish was still not great, so we must have looked funny to the locals. We were going everywhere asking "Donde es el huachumero Martin?" The original name for San Pedro is Huachuma (or Wachuma) and shamans who heal with the cactus are sometimes called huachumero's. After a couple of hours of looking around for him we decided to give up for the day and try again tomorrow. We were relaxing in our room watching TV in Spanish when there was a knock at our hotel room door. It was 9:30 at night and we were totally confused. I answered the door and there was a short Peruvian man looking up at me. Suddenly he says, "Hola, I am Martin. Would you like to drink San Pedro tomorrow?" We were totally blown away! He had found us!

The next morning he took us to his house and showed us his altar for ceremony. He said some prayers and blew tobacco smoke on us as we drank the medicine, and then he walked us over to the temple and took us inside. Martin had grown up living in the temple with his grandmother until the government asked him to move out the year before – they wanted to start inviting tourists to the center and kicked him out. You could tell how much the temple meant to him and how dear it was to his heart.

He gave us a lot of time to meditate in different parts of the temple, and Tasha went really deep in her ceremony. She told me that she had gone back in time and saw the temple when it was full of people. San Pedro showed her how he had taught all these people about astronomy, healing and art.

We had a great time with Martin and really appreciated his guidance and his beautiful ceremony. After seeing him we had another week in Peru and we slowly made our way back to the coast and enjoyed the free time together.

Q'ero History and Cosmology

The Q'ero natives are a tribe from the remote high Andes. There are no roads to their villages – you have to walk or take a donkey 3 days from the nearest road to reach where they live. For a long time the modern world didn't really know about the Q'ero – they lived so remotely that only a few hacienda owners who treated them like slaves were aware of them. Since the modern world was virtually ignorant of their existence, most of their history before the 1950's is only known through the stories and oral traditions of the Q'ero themselves.

There is enough evidence to confirm that the Q'ero were once part of the Inka empire. What their role in that empire was is uncertain. The Q'ero claim that when the Spanish arrived and killed the Inkarri – the Inka King – that the whole Q'ero's people fled high into the mountains to hide and remain free. A small group of the Spanish invaders followed them but a great Q'ero priest called on the mountain spirits to protect them and the mountain spirit caused some sort of avalanche that killed the Spanish who chased the Q'ero. The Q'ero went high into the remote mountains and were left alone because no one else could chase them or survive long at that high altitude, and eventually they were forgotten. The rest of the Inka empire thought that the Q'ero were extinct.

That high in the mountains life is very harsh. It is hard to grow food and make a living, but the Q'ero are extremely hard working and resilient. They also have very powerful priests who they call paqo's. The word paqo means something like a priest or practitioner. While the Q'ero spiritual practice in many ways looks shamanic many claim they are not technically shamans because they do not use altered states to work with spirits (no drumming or plant medicines ect). Instead they call the spirits – this is an animistic practice. One benefit of living so remotely and secretly in the mountains is that the Q'ero had almost zero contact with the modern world and Catholic European culture – more than any Andean culture the Q'ero are known for still living the same way they have for thousands of years. This is why they are considered some of the most authentic and traditional Andean healers, and because their traditional ways are so powerful they are highly sought out as teachers by other healers in the area.

In the 1950's the Q'ero decided to come out of hiding. I mentioned that there were a few hacienda owners who treated them like slaves – the Q'ero were being abused and decided they needed help from the outside world to free themselves from this servitude. They also had prophecies that said they were to teach and share their culture and spiritual practices with the modern world. So they came to the festival of Q'olloriti'l where an anthropologist recognized their hand-woven clothes as being of Inka origin. Because the Spanish had destroyed the local culture and practices these weaving patterns had been lost and were only seen in museums – but the Q'ero still knew how to make them and were all wearing them. If you ever see these woven patterns they are extremely high quality and very intricate – all done by hand and without following any pattern, just making each one unique from the weavers mind.

Since then many people have been learning from the Q'ero and incorporating their traditions into the other local practices. A lot of the shamanic practices in Peru can have a Catholic influence because of the close relationship with the Spanish invaders for 500 years. Many shamans included Catholic rites so that they could continue to practice in a land where the Spanish would kill anyone practicing paganism. This would be for example one of the reasons that the cactus Wachuma was renamed San Pedro after Saint Peter – when the locals were taught about the saints and heard St. Peter holds the keys to heaven they thought St. Peter must really be Wachuma! And so they changed the name as a way to avoid persecution by making the medicine sound more Catholic. Because of the heavy Spanish influence on indigenous cultures it had become hard to tell what practices were traditional Peruvian and which were Catholic influenced, but with the Q'ero people could learn how to return back to their roots a little bit.

As we keep discussing the Q'ero cosmology and practice one thing I want to point out is that the Q'ero have no dogmatic beliefs and no organized religion. They do not all necessarily agree on everything or tell the same stories and prophecies. They do not all practice exactly the same. There is quite a bit of variety and if you ask two different Q'ero shamans about one subject it is totally possible to get conflicting answers from both of them. They have a few core values which guide their morals and lifestyle, but other than that they can often have unique beliefs. So when I discuss their cosmology, this is only coming from my personal understanding and what I have heard from the Q'ero I know. If you read something different in a book or see them doing something different in person – this wouldn't surprise me because there is a lot of variety in their tradition.

The Q'ero have two different levels of paqo: pampa mesayok and alta mesayok. They also work predominantly with mountain spirits (called "Apu's" as in "Apu Ausangate") as well as Pachamama (the cosmic mother which might mean the whole universe, or may mean just the Earth or "Mother Nature"), and they also work heavily with the Sun (Inti TayTay), the moon (Mama Killa), the stars (hatun chaska or "star people") and the ocean (Mama Qocha). Their language is Quechua which was spoken by the Inka empire.

Like many shamanic cultures the Q'ero also believe in and work with the 3 worlds – they call the upper world "Hanaq Pacha," the middle world is "Kay Pacha" or "Kawsay Pacha," and the lower world is the "Uchu Pacha." These worlds are also often represented by different animals – the lower world is represented by the serpent Amaru (or sometimes also called Sachamama), the middle world by the puma Hatun Puma, and the upper world is most often represented by the condor (Apu Kontor, Apuchin, or Apuchina), though sometimes it is also represented by the hummingbird Sawai'kinti. The 3 worlds and the 4 directions are often represented by a symbol called the "chakana" or "Andean Cross."

Ukhu translates as "inner, interior or deep." Pacha is basically translated as world or space and time. So the Ukhu Pacha is the lower world. This is a place you can journey to for maturity and growth to take place. It contains both Sami and Hucha and it is a place where Ayni is not yet realized – so here we can learn Ayni and bring ourselves into a deeper relationship with the world around us. Here we can encounter our own shadow selves and unconscious minds so that we can learn and grow and heal. Here you can heal soul loss, and here you can come to die so that you may be reborn. The serpent symbolizes this world because it sheds its past to be reborn and because it lives belly to belly with the earth and in holes that go underground.

Kay translates as "this" or "to be or exist". Kawsay is the living energy within everything. So the Kawsay Pacha is our world – the middle world. All energies and influences meet within this world – the Kawsay Pacha is connected to everything. This is where we can learn lessons and apply that knowledge to our everyday lives. The Puma or Jaguar represents this world because of the strength and presence these animals carry.

Hanaq Pacha is the upper world – Hanaq translates as "above or over" and Hanaq Pacha together means something like "highest world." This is where the most evolved states of consciousness live and this world is comprised completely of Sami (light energy) – no Hucha (heavy energy) or disharmony exists here. You can journey here to bring back awakened blessings to the Kay Pacha. The condor or the eagle represents this world because it flies higher than other birds and can carry the prayers of the people to the heavens. Interestingly enough, there is also an interesting relationship between the condor and the puma where the puma will watch the condor circling weakened animals and know it has easy prey there. When the puma kills the injured animal it will leave some of the meat for the condor otherwise the condor will stop helping it hunt. So the puma uses the condor for guidance just as we can look to the heavens of guidance, and the puma always respects the love of the upper world by giving something back in reciprocation.

The Q'ero also have a number of defining principles and values which guide their lives. The first is that everything has its own living energy and is a part of a greater whole – they call this energy kawsay. The other main guiding principles are as follows:

Ayni – Reciprocation. When you give you must receive and when you receive you must give. Everything is constantly exchanging energy and the more you connect with and give to the world around you, the more you will receive. To give freely and to be open to receiving requires trust, and this is a key for exchanging energy. This is the basis for example, of making offerings to the spirits to have prayers answered. Another beautiful aspect of this belief is that instead of trying to make profits or get a better deal than people you do business with – you instead seek to find a fair and equal exchange where everyone benefits. All exchanges and connections with others are based on this principal of reciprocity. A perfect example of reciprocation with the world around us is when you breathe – exchanging air with the world around you and changing oxygen to carbon dioxide, which a tree will then breath and turn back into oxygen for you.

With Living Energy (Kawsay) making up the world around us and reciprocation (Ayni) connecting us all, there are 3 powers to help you move energy and come into deeper reciprocation with the world around you. Yachay is the power of the mind, Llank'ay is the power of the body, and Munay is the power of love which can be used to move Kawsay. Kawsay is the living energy all around us, so moving Kawsay means you can move energy like Sami and Hucha.

Munay – More specifically than love, Munay is directed or intentional love. Learning how to develop a strong sense of unconditional and intentional love for the world around you can help you move more Kawsay. Munay is built through trust, acceptance and caring as well as acts of kindness and generosity.

Yanantin – Harmonious relationship between compliments. The celebration of diversity. All differences are beneficial and complimentary. Energy is neither good nor bad, but instead heavy or light, and all energy is useful. Energies working together are life-affirming and create more Munay and Ayni.

Yachay – Power of knowledge and the mind. To learn, to know and to remember. Learning from the experience of others and passing down this knowledge to those who come after you. Also being flexible in your thinking to allow more learning.

Llank'ay – Power of action and work. This is not only physical work, but mental work, creative and artistic work, and even healing work. Ceremonial and conscious lifestyle imbues work with meaning and for the Q'ero ceremony and work always go together. When they plant a new crop they do it with ceremony, and when they harvest the same crop they do it with ceremony. This brings new awareness and appreciation to your work and lifestyle.

It was mentioned before that Munay, Yachay and Llank'ay are synergistically connected. Love and beauty (Munay) make daily living pleasing and soften the hard edges of difficulties. Without initiating right action (Llank'ay) nothing gets done and things stagnate. Action for its own sake can lead to conflict, however - the best outcome of action proceeds from knowledge (Yachay).

As one learns and grows, each principle transforms into a higher form. Munay becomes deeper impersonal love that embraces all things. Yachay becomes the superior consciousness one arrives at through the proper cultivation of love and work. Llank'ay is not just work and routine ritual, but becomes right livelihood. A conscious way of living that promotes the welfare of others and encourages service performed in the spirit of loving kindness.

These principles can also be thought of as the ability to feel (Munay), think (Yachay), and act (Llank'ay). Just to work, just to think, and to be consumed by one's emotions is imbalanced. When in harmony, these principles balance an individual. According to Q'ero belief, for one to be at peace and happy it is necessary to harmonize these in your manner and daily life. Only when the emotions, thoughts, and actions are aligned can you be a balanced human.

These foundational beliefs are a large part of what drew me to the Q'ero. If you ever spend time with them you can see how their belief system has led them to their current culture and spiritual practice, and they are the most humble, caring and peaceful people you could ever find. I think these values also represent a deeper spiritual tradition... Sometimes in practical spirituality like shamanism people can lose sight of what is really important. Yes, healing and getting practical help in life is very good, but there is also a deeper spirituality of personal experience and love and connection and altruism that sometimes gets overlooked. I am really inspired by traditions that focus on how to be a good loving person who tries to leave the Earth better then they found it.

I mentioned before that the Q'ero do not use trance states from plants or drumming to communicate with spirits. Instead their ceremony focuses heavily on long improvised prayers, offerings to Pachamama and the Apu's, working with a style of altar called a mesa, and working with condor feathers. They also use different stones for energy work and may do ceremony in temples or power spots in nature. They really work with nature spirits and the medicine of nature in a very grounded and old traditional way. Even though they don't use plants to reach altered states it should be mentioned that they highly revere the Coca plant and will often chew it every day. They chew the plant for food and to help with work, but also as a form of prayer and they even use it in offerings – the Coca plant is integral to their culture.

When the Q'ero talk about working with energy and moving or pushing energy, they designate these energies into "light energy" (Sami) or "heavy energy" (Hucha). Sami can also be translated as nectar – energy that feeds and sustains us. Hucha is dense energy that has become out of harmony or out of balance – the Q'ero do not think of this energy as negative or bad, but just as energy that needs to be rebalanced and transformed back into harmony. Many times Hucha is caused by repressed emotions, traumas, environmental or energetic pollution, dark thoughts and so on... Healers will cleanse Hucha and replace it with Sami to help restore health and balance to the body, mind and spirit. When the Hucha is cleansed it is done in a way so that it may become Sami once again – often times the paqo's will give the Hucha to Mother Earth or the Mother Ocean to transmute back into Sami.

From the Q'ero view a person's body also has certain energetic centers which can be used for moving energy, and which can also become imbalanced if too much Hucha accumulates. The first part of this energy body is called the poqpo – it is an egg shaped energy field around your body that most people would call an aura. There are also 5 energy centers called "chunpi's" which are similar in some ways to chakras. Chunpi is a Quechua word for "belt" and these energy centers are described as 5 belts around your body with "eye's" in the center of each one called a "nawi." The eyes line up in a line down your core in the same locations as your root, solar plexus, heart, throat and third eye chakras (there is no nawi/chunpi at the sacral chakra or crown chakra). The chunpi's are as follows:

- Yana Chunpi (root chakra – black). The eye for this chunpi is siki nawi. It is associated with the element of water and the spirit Mama Qocha.

- Puka Chunpi (sacral and solar plexus chakras – red). Qosco nawi. Earth/Pachamama.

- Qori Chunpi (heart – golden). Sonqo Nawi ("eye of the heart"). Inti Taytay and fire.

- Qolqe Chunpi (throat – silver). Kunka Nawi. Wind and Mama Killa.

- Kulli Chunpi (third eye and both regular eyes are 3 nawi's which combine to make this one belt/chunpi – violet). Third eye is called Qanchis Nawi. Connects you to Source or Creator.

One chunpi in particular deserves a special mention. This is the Puka Chunpi located at the solar plexus. Its nawi is called the qosqo and this is the most important energy center used by paqo's to push Kawsay. Qosqo is the Quechua word for "naval" and can also be spelled "Cusco." The city of Cusco is considered in Peru to be the naval of the universe and of Pachamama.

These chunpi's are special energy centers that can be used in meditation to cleanse your energy or someone else's energy, or to connect with different energies around you. There are even special stones designed for performing energy work on the chunpi's called "chunpi khuya's" (khuya is a magical stone used for healing).

Q'ero Based Meditations

I mentioned before that the Q'ero have many different rites and practices and that not all of them practice the same rituals. These are a few meditations for personal energetic hygiene as well as for developing personal power and connection to the energies of nature around you. I don't know how widely these meditations are used throughout the Q'ero tradition but they seem pretty common. They are for the most part very straight forward and easy, though if practiced with openness and trust on a regular basis they can be powerful and transformative.

SAMINCHAKUY: Releasing Hucha

This is a personal meditation to help you release your Hucha as well as help you connect to Sami from the Upper World (Hanaq Pacha). I have seen it taught a few slightly different ways, but the core of the practice is always the same. This meditation is based solely on intention, trust and letting go – it is very simple to practice if you can trust the process. If you get too in your head about it you can block the flow of energy, so as much as you can try to just go with it.

You start by finding a good spot for your meditation. It can really be done anywhere and anytime once you get it down, but it is especially effective if you can try this somewhere in nature while sitting on the ground. The practice is generally easier when you sit on the floor or ground somewhere. Begin by centering yourself and taking a few deep breaths. Take a moment to tune into your poqpo – feel its boundary about a foot from your body. Notice how the poqpo feels to you and if you sense anything about your energies current state. Slowly shift your awareness to the world around you and up to the heavens. Remember you are connected to all life and energy. Also try to be aware of the top of your poqpo and a connection from your crown up to the heavens. With your intention and trust ask the Hanaq Pacha to give you its Sami and let this Sami flow in through the top of your poqpo and fill your entire being. This creates a column of light from the heavens o your body. Feel the energy fill your head, your chest, your arms and legs…. As you feel it course through your entire body and fill you completely – take a moment to enjoy this feeling.

Then slowly start to shift your awareness to underneath you. Feel your connection to the Earth and feel your poqpo connect with Pachamama. Ask Pachamama to take your Hucha and tell your body to release its Hucha to the Earth. Release your Hucha as a sacred gift to the Earth – remember that Hucha is not bad energy. Just like when you breathe out carbon dioxide, you are exchanging energy with another spirit who benefits from this exchange. Hucha is like food to Mother Earth – she eats Hucha and digests it, turning it back into Sami and life. Think about how a plant or animal can die or leave its waste behind and the Earth will take nutrients from its decomposing body or waste and turn those nutrients into more life – this process is similar to that. You and the Earth both benefit from this exchange. Keep releasing Hucha until you feel the flow of energy slow down and you have a sense of relief.

If you feel light and free after this experience – great! If you feel a headache or any discomfort then this is also a good sign – you have released blockages that desensitize you to your own discomfort and this is part of the healing process.

Sometimes it is nice to repeat the process a couple times starting again by receiving Sami from the Hanaq Pacha and then releasing more Hucha to the Earth. Trust your intuition on how many times to repeat.

When you first practice this meditation it is good to spend 5-10 minutes releasing your Hucha. As you get more experienced and have already worked through a lot of your Hucha you may find that you only need a few minutes or even just a few seconds for this practice. We always pick up Hucha in our day to day lives, so this is a regular cleaning practice kind of like an energetic shower – it is good to do this meditation every day when you are able, though it can be a helpful practice no matter the frequency. The practice is also especially helpful when you have troubles – maybe you get in a argument with someone or let your emotions get carried away – this meditation can really help bring you back to center.

I have seen other variations on this that I would like to mention. While I explained this as a process starting with receiving Sami and then afterwards

174

releasing Hucha, some people reverse the order. Some people also do them at the same time. I think this is a personal preference and you can do it the way that feels best to you.

SAYWAYCHAKUY: Reciprocate The Energy

This meditation should always follow the releasing Hucha exercise. You remember the principal of Ayni (reciprocation)? To receive you must give, and when you give you also receive. Since we offered to Pachamama we can now receive her Sami, and because we received Sami from the Hanaq Pacha we should reciprocate by giving Sami back to them. This completes the cycle of Ayni and energy exchange.

Begin by tuning back into your poqpo and feeling your connection to Mother Earth. As you feel that connection ask her to send you Sami and allow yourself to receive that Sami. Let the Sami fill your being from the Earth up into your entire body. As it fills you add your own Sami to it – your gratitude and love, and then offer this combined Sami to the Hanaq Pacha. This creates a new column of light from the Earth, through you, and up to the heavens. Let this energy flow for as long as it feels right. When you are done take a moment to tune into your body – how do you feel? I also like to take a second and silently thank Pachamama and the Hanaq Pacha for exchanging and sharing their energy with you.

......

One thing I really liked when I learned these two meditations was how similar they are to something the plant medicines and nature had taught me before. I remember the first time I went backpacking was also the first time I tried mushrooms in the forest. I was camping in the old growth of the Hoh Rainforest with a good friend and after a dip in some natural hot springs we ate mushrooms and went on a hike to an alpine lake on top of the mountain. My intention at the time was for the mushrooms to connect me to the earth and to nature – and boy did I get what I asked for!

As my friend and I were hiking the mountain itself started talking to me! It told me that I could give all my pain and disharmonious energies to it and that I wouldn't hurt it. It showed me how all things live and die on this mountain – the trees and deer and bears…. The mountain takes their pain and their death and turns it back into life. So the mountain told me to give it my pain, and as I let go I could feel the energy leaving me and going into the mountain with every step. I had never heard of Hucha or the Q'ero at the time – but I was releasing Hucha!

When I learned the Q'ero practice I was blown away by how similar it was to my own experience with the mountain that day, and also excited to take the practice another step further by adding the acceptance of Sami and the reciprocal exchange of energy. I also found it easier to accept and believe in these Q'ero practices because they seemed so similar to what came to me naturally through experience.

On the topic of Sami and Hucha I want to return to some of the Q'ero philosophies on energy. Remember that Sami and Hucha are not good or bad – they are just different frequencies of energy. Hucha may be harmful to humans, but it is food to the Earth, so its nature is neither good nor bad – it just is. Some energies are light and the others heavier, and there can be grades in-between the two. Some Hucha is heavier than other Hucha. And what is Hucha for one person might not be Hucha for someone else. I was told one story about the Q'ero where an apprentice was sitting on a tall rock and releasing his Hucha when he realized his teacher was right below him where his Hucha was going to! He apologized to the teacher and felt bad he had sent Hucha to his teacher, but his teacher just laughed and replied, "What makes you think your Hucha isn't Sami for me?"

Because the Q'ero do not see energy as good or bad, they also don't see things in terms of good and evil. They see some things as being out of harmony and possibly destructive, but something out of harmony can always be brought back into harmony, and its inner nature is not seen as objectively evil – just out of harmony. When someone does something to cause pain to another the Q'ero assume the person either did not know any better, or they assume that the person has some trauma or trouble causing them to be out of harmony and that disharmony inspires them to act destructively. By healing and bringing the self back into harmony they can transmute the Hucha into Sami and the person can return to a balanced state.

When you stop seeing things in terms of good or bad opposites and start seeing them as compliments that can harmonize you can shift a lot about your life. The Q'ero talk about 3 stages of a relationship which they call tinkuy (encounter), tupay (conflict, challenge, competition) and taqe (joining/harmonizing). When two people found themselves in a competition there is a rule that whoever wins the competition must teach the other competitor how they won! This is an example of how a community focused world-view based on harmony can be beneficial.

More Advanced Q'ero Energy Work

There are many styles of energy work the Q'ero might do. They cleanse Hucha using feathers and palo santo or Agua de Florida, they move Kawsay with their mesa altars or with offerings to the Earth and mountain spirits, they use crystals and prayers... But first we will continue learning about energy practices using just your body.

Working with your Qosqo

The Qosqo is the most important energy center in the Q'ero tradition. It is located at your navel and is the "eye" of the Puka Chunpi. To start working with your Qosqo it is good to practice feeling and sensing it, and then using it to "taste" different energies. The more you use your Qosqo the stronger it will get – just like working out a muscle.

Begin by using your hand to sense your qosqo. This is the easiest way to first sense it, and afterwards you can eventually do all of this without your hands but just your intention and awareness. Hold a hand in front of your naval about 6 inches – if you feel with your hand you should be able to find the sensation of an energy center right in front of your naval. That is your qosqo. If you don't feel it right away trying moving your open palm closer and further from your body slowly – in the range of 4-7 inches until you get a sense of where it is at. Don't get in your head too much or doubt yourself – trust your feelings!

When you have a sense of your qosqo you can experiment with opening and closing it. With your hand still in front of your qosqo, rotate your hand counter-clockwise (from your perspective) and forward – pulling the qosqo open and out with it (it widens as it opens and you can widen your hand rotations with that opening). To close it rotate the opposite way. This is the most basic level of control with your qosqo – you can open it more when you want it to be more sensitive and open, and close it if you want to be less sensitive. Generally it rests at a semi-closed state when not being used.

Your qosqo also has tendrils or filaments of light that can reach out of it. These are like threads of energy that you can use to touch and taste other energies. To direct them you only need to use your intention – they will follow where you tell them to go and where you focus on. So if you want to test or taste a certain energy you can tell your qosqo to reach these threads out and touch the object, and then to "eat" or "taste" a tiny bit of its energy.

To start practicing with your qosqo and tasting energies choose objects you think of as having lots of Sami and good energy, and don't work with objects which seem to have Hucha just yet – you want to develop your senses and the strength of your qosqo before trying denser energies. Some good energies to start tasting with might be a favorite tree, a favorite rock, the sun, moon, stars…. It can be especially insightful to spend a week or a month tasting the sun or moon daily during different set times so that you can develop your relationship with those spirits as well as develop and sensitize your sense of taste. Try tasting the sun at sunrise, sunset, high noon, and even at night when you cannot see it. Try tasting it when it is behind clouds and when it is in the open. Taste it during different seasons of the year. Do the same with the moon and try tasting it during different moon phases as well. Notice the subtle differences in their energies and think about what that means to you. You might not notice many differences at first, but as you practice you will be able to distinguish these energies better and learn more from tasting with your qosqo.

If you ever taste an energy that makes you feel sick or not quite right – stop right away and release Hucha to the Earth. It might be too dense for you to safely work with at this time, but as your qosqo develops strength through your continued practice you should eventually be able to come back to it.

Hucha Mikuy

Similar to the practices of releasing Hucha and receiving Sami, there is also a practice called *Hucha Mikuy* which is based on *digesting* Hucha and turning it into Sami. Just like your body can digest food and separate out the waste and nutrients, your energy body can digest energy and separate the Hucha and Sami. You take the Sami into your body and offer the Hucha to Mother Earth.

This practice is done with your qosqo. Your qosqo will digest Hucha the same way your stomach would digest food – it will separate the nutrients (Sami) from the waste (Hucha) and the nutrients will go to your body while the rest you give back to mother Earth (just like when you eat and eliminate the waste after).

The first time you practice this it is best to work on yourself first. After practicing on yourself a number of times you can then start also practicing on people you get along with really well. Once you have much more practice and the strength of your qosqo is more developed you can also use this practice to help clean people who are sick or have other heavy energies and can even use it to cleanse objects and places. If two people are in conflict you can even digest the Hucha between them that is causing the conflict. But you want to start off with easy and safe people or objects and give yourself time to work up to more challenging ones. If you ever are digesting Hucha and start to feel not right, stop and release Hucha.

To start with yourself begin by sensing your energy and body. Do you feel like a certain place could use some attention or cleaning? Maybe you can feel some Hucha there, or just get a sense that would be a good spot to work. Tell the threads in your qosqo to reach out to that spot on your body and tell it to start digesting Hucha. In some ways this is a little similar to tasting an energy with your qosqo, but you will draw in more energy and specifically aim for drawing in Hucha. Try to imagine in your minds eyes that your qosqo filaments are drawing in this energy and that your qosqo is digesting it – tell your body to do this and it will know how.

You will know you are doing this right when you feel a line of energy coming into your naval and that line splits into two lines: a line of Sami going up to your crown area and a line of Hucha going down to Mother Earth. If you don't feel those separate lines try telling your body to separate the energies and try to imagine them splitting in the way described. You can use your imagination and trust to guide the energies. Because you are releasing Hucha to Pachamama it can be nice to sit on the ground while doing this practice, but it is not necessary.

Continue the practice until you feel it slow down on its own, or until you feel like it is time to stop.

Afterwards you may feel like that was enough and you are now finished, or you may feel like you want to do the regular releasing Hucha practice to finish up with (and of course the meditation of reciprocation done after releasing Hucha).

YANANCHAKUY: weaving complementary living energies with a partner

Find a partner who you feel comfortable with. Eventually it is fun to try this with many different partners to have different experiences. Before beginning the Yananchakuy first practice Saminchakuy and Saywachakuy (releasing Hucha and reciprocation). This way you both work on your own energies before combining your energies and start from a clean slate.

Start by standing back to back with a little space between you – maybe about a foot apart. Next decide who wants to move their energy earthward and wants to move it skyward – I will refer to these as EW and SW for simplicity. EW place your right hand on the top of your head and your left hand on your sacrum. SW will place the left hand on top of the head and the right and the sacrum. Your right hands will be active and the left receptive.

EW open the top of your poqpo and receive the finest Sami from the Hanaq Pacha into the top of your head. With your intention send a pulse of energy from your right hand on top of your head down your spine to the hand on your sacrum. SW open the bottom of your poqpo and receive Sami from Pachamama and use your right hand to send that energy up your spine to the left hand on top of your head. Once you both feel that you have a stream of energy moving from your right hand to your left hand you can let your hands down by your sides and put your backs together – not leaning on each other but just barely touching or close to touching.

EW keep pulling Sami down your spine, but then send it from your sacrum to your partners sacrum. SW you will receive the Sami through your sacrum and channel it up your spine and from your head into your partners head where they will receive it – the two of you are creating a cycle here. While you are doing this you can keep pulling in Sami from the Hanaq Pacha and Pachamama as well and keep mixing into the Sami you are both circulating. It might take a few seconds to really feel the circuit moving freely, but try to focus and keep it going for 4-5 minutes until you feel your energies harmonizing. When you are done you can both take a step apart and face each other and share your experiences.

NAWI KICHAY: Opening Nawi - Chunpi Meditations

Start by bringing your awareness first into your body and your qosqo, and when you feel ready move your awareness down to the base of your spine until you get a sense of your Siki Nawi (the eye of your base chunpi). With your Munay and intention ask this eye to open and reach out to the nearest body of water (if no water is near then reach into the earth seeking ground water). Release your nawi's Hucha to this body of water, and when you are done receive the Sami from this body of water – let that Sami fill your Siki Nawi first and once that is full let the excess Sami go up your spine to your crown (enjoy this flow of Sami till you feel finished).

You will repeat the steps of opening each Nawi and releasing Hucha, then drinking in Sami. Your Qosqo at the naval will connect with the Earth. Your Sonqo Nawi at the heart will connect with the Sun. The Kunka Nawi at the throat will connect with the moon, and the 3 Nawi's associated with your "third eye" area will connect with Creator and the Upper World.

Once you have cleaned and empowered each of your Nawi's/Chunpi's you can harmonize them together. Start at the Kulli Chunpi of your third eye and ask that energy to harmonize with your throat chunpi. Then ask the throat chunpi to harmonize with the heart chunpi. Then ask the heart to harmonize with the naval chunpi, and finally the naval to harmonize with the chunpi at your sacrum. When all of these chunpi's and nawi's have harmonized you can then release any leftover Hucha to Mother Earth to finish this practice.

Sharing the Plants

"It's the possibility of having a dream come true that makes life interesting." ~ The Alchemist

When Tasha and I returned home from our wedding and second trip to Peru I was thinking about what San Pedro had told me at Lesley's. Two years in a row San Pedro had suggested I share his medicine with others. I didn't have a traditional apprenticeship but I did have a lot of personal experience and I had seen and understood how Lesley was working in Cusco.... I thought I could do something kind of similar but with my own twist, but at the same time I also felt like it was irresponsible to offer medicine without specific training in serving it. Lesley had told me that her apprenticeship consisted of drinking San Pedro twice a week for 2 years straight, and while I had about 8 years of experience with plant medicines and had started drinking San Pedro about 6 years before, I thought maybe I should just order and start drinking tons of San Pedro all of the time and see where that led. Almost like my own solitary apprenticeship. I couldn't afford to move to Peru or sit in that many ceremonies – it costs a lot of money and I was totally broke after our travels.... So I thought this might be the best option in the meantime and I could see where it led.

So I ordered a giant box of San Pedro from a good local source. Luckily San Pedro cactus is legal to buy and sell where I was so it was easy to get. I ordered this large box expecting it to last me many ceremonies so I could get a lot of learning under my belt. As soon as I clicked order, my phone rang. Do you remember when I mentioned a friend named "Steve" who decided to skip our last Peru trip because he wasn't ready to be happy yet? Well it was him on the phone. I hadn't seen him in years and had only talked to him briefly when he wanted to come to our wedding and last Peru trip – he lived on the other side of the country in Georgia and we didn't talk much. He told me that he was incredibly depressed and feeling suicidal. He had a rash on his head that would burst open and ooze puss, he was battling alcohol addiction and his girlfriend had just slept with his best friend on his birthday. He kept trying new doctors and different treatments but everything the doctors did made his depression worse, his rash worse, and he was feeling lost and helpless. He didn't know why, but he had this feeling like Tasha and I could help him for some reason and he asked if he could come visit. I told him that I had no clue how to help him, but I was always there to support him and he could visit anytime he liked. He asked if he could show up in 3 days – he had miles left from the plane ticket he canceled when he decided to skip Peru. I looked at the confirmation order from the San Pedro I had just bought. It was supposed to arrive in 3 days – right when Steve wanted to come. Coincidence? Or a friendly nudge from San Pedro? I told Steve showing up in 3 days was fine, and I started planning how I might try to help him out a bit.

Now at this time I had experience healing my own depression, experience with plant medicines, and experience with energy work and some types of healing – but I had never tried to organize a plant medicine ceremony for anyone other than Tasha and myself. I had ideas about how to do it – how to be safe, how to help someone through a difficult experience with the medicine, how to format a ceremony and bring lots of prayer and intention to the whole process.... But I had no clue if it would help or benefit someone else. I knew it worked for Tasha and me, and I knew how Lesley formatted her ceremonies to help people and she got great results.... But she had apprenticed to a San Pedro shaman for 2 years. I had 8 years of experience with healing, psychedelics and spirituality – but no traditional apprenticeship. Would the miracle of the medicine speak through the plants for us? I wasn't sure, but I knew Steve needed help, and I had a lot of faith in San Pedro.

I felt like I didn't really know how to help Steve – I had ideas, but they hadn't been tested yet. But I knew San Pedro had powerful medicine and I knew the redwoods had a lot of magic and wonder. I thought if I combined the magic of both that we would have the best chance of deep healing. If I didn't know how to help him I was convinced that nature knew how and so we made a plan to really open ourselves up to the wisdom of the Earth. Steve showed up for 2 weeks and I asked if he was open to a 10 day camping trip in the redwoods. He loved the idea. I told him about San Pedro and how it helps many people and had taught me a lot. I told him I wasn't any shaman, but San Pedro is a wonderful healer and if he wanted to try it out that I would do my best to support him during ceremony and that with a little luck maybe he would see benefits. I made no promises but told him this could be worth a try – almost like an experiment. He thought it was worth a shot as well, so Tasha, Steve and me all packed and left for the redwoods. We brought enough brewed San Pedro for the 3 of us to do 2 ceremonies, and I also brought some magic mushrooms since those had helped my depression so much. I was nervous about sharing medicine with Steve, but he had worked with psychedelics in the past and he felt like this was the best option for him since at this point he had seen a dozen doctors and tried every other treatment for his depression with no positive results.

It's about a 10 hour drive to the redwoods so we had a lot of time to talk. Steve told me about his depression, how it affects him, and how he had attempted to treat it in the past. Doctors had given him all kinds of drugs and medications and he had seen all kinds of therapy – many of the drugs had made his depression worse, and nothing had helped him so far. Doctors had also tried to treat the mysterious rash he had had for years – most treatments had made that worse as well. Doctors had no clue what was causing it or how to fix it – I wondered if it might be linked to his depression and sort of an auto-immune psychosomatic illness…. I knew many stories of plant medicines curing illnesses that doctors had no luck with so I was hopeful and curious. Doctors were unable to help him and so far had mostly made the issue worse, so Steve felt this was his only hope.

In the redwoods the three of us did four ceremonies. Two with San Pedro and two with the mushrooms. We started with San Pedro and alternated the medicines as we worked – the four ceremonies were spread out over eight days so we always had a day off in-between to integrate and relax. With the mushrooms we would take long hikes into the forest, and with San Pedro we would stay a little closer to camp and spend most of our time relaxing on the beach or in the forest close to camp. We always started our ceremonies by calling in the directions, making an offering, saying some prayers and setting a clear intention. We had lots of time for quiet reflection and listening to the plants, and sometimes I would also have to talk with Steve to help him work through the difficult periods. We let our intuition guide us as we did ceremony – we would stop at special trees to meditate, I practiced the hollow bone idea and would suggest Steve climbed through hallow scary looking logs to be reborn on the other side.... I let the forest become part of our ceremony and let it inspire me on how to connect with it for healing. At one point I channeled an icaro that sounded like Shipibo and Steve said it opened up a portal that he went through to memories from his childhood.... The ceremonies were challenging, but it always felt like the plants were guiding me and telling me how to support Steve.

With San Pedro things went very smoothly – the cactus brought him so much light and very practical insights. The mushrooms were purging his darkness – which means they would bring it all to the surface for him to deal with and let go of. It was heartbreaking seeing how hard Steve was on himself, but I felt a true sense of mission striving to love him through the whole process and support his healing. The mushroom ceremonies were a bit more intense and I had to do a lot more supporting and guiding, whereas the cactus did all the work on its own as long as I gave him space to connect with it. Overall the ceremonies were all helpful in their own way and while 4 ceremonies was not enough to resolve all of Steve's issues, he did call me a month later to say that there were some positive changes. We stayed in contact since then and while he didn't have another opportunity to come do more work with me, I was able to notice large shifts in his personality – he would still get depressed and beat himself up emotionally – but he would catch himself and change it quickly whereas before he would just stew in it. His rash wasn't completely gone but was much less intense – actually the best since when he had first started having it. I wish we had more time together and that we could have helped him more, but I was still really happy to see the benefits and to have spent that time with him. Years later I still remember that camping trip as one of my favorites.

After Steve went home I did a lot more experimenting on my own and with friends. I ended up doing ceremonies very regularly and learning a lot over the next few years. As I got more experience the ceremonies improved and soon I developed my own style and started learning many icaros and medicine songs from the plants – it was as if I had apprenticed to the plants and was learning from them directly. It was difficult and challenging – I had many doubts and had to put a lot of thought and effort into how to do this safely and effectively. I was heavily inspired and influenced by what I learned each year in Peru, and from that foundation I was learning the rest through personal experience. Eventually I even decided to guide personal ceremonies for others using local legal entheogens like tobacco, Salvia Divinorum and Amanita Muscaria.

I ended up sharing experiences with many other people that taught me a lot about the power of the plant medicines. One lady I shared ceremony with went from having 2-4 panic attacks every week to having zero in only a single ceremony. Another lady went from having migraines almost daily to having none after her first ever experience. Someone else healed their frozen shoulder which had bothered them for 20 years, but in one afternoon with San Pedro they completely healed. Something was working. We were doing something right.

Now I don't think the path I ended up following is necessarily the best for everyone. Learning to host ceremonies on your own I think is actually much harder than learning from a teacher, and in my case I don't think I could have done it without learning from the shamans I met in Peru. Even though I hadn't formally apprenticed to anyone I had learned a lot from them still, and they showed me what level of competence I needed to responsibly offer these ceremonies. Even after having many success's I still wanted to apprentice and learn more – I just couldn't even come close to being able to afford anything like that. I made the best with what I had and more than anything I made sure that everyone was always safe when with me. It is unacceptable for anyone to go home from my ceremony worse of then when they arrived – if they don't find healing I can handle that, but no one should ever be harmed in any way.

I felt guided to this work from my near death experience in the ocean, through my own personal healing, through years of practice and study, and though some friendly nudges from the plants. I learned as much as I could – energy work, psychology, science of the plants and how they work, how traditional shamans host ceremonies…. And I had years of personal work with the plant medicines under my belt. I sometimes see people with only a couple ceremonies under their belt and zero experience doing other healing work attempt to host ceremonies and I get pretty worried. A lot more goes into it then that. I was even worried to host for others after I had worked with plants for 8 years and experienced thousands of ceremonies. Please – don't jump into this work before you are ready.

At the same time.... This has worked for me. It took me a long time to get to the point where I could do this work – 8 years before I started hosting a few people, and about 6 months of experimenting and testing with that before I really opened my doors. I also know of a famous Peruvian shaman who had no teacher and is regarded as one of the best healers in Peru – he went into the jungle for 2 years on his own and dieted in isolation without a teacher – when he came back he was a healer. But after following this path and meeting many other healers – I would say we are the exceptions to the rule.... It is best when possible if you can find a teacher. If it isn't possible to formally apprentice there are other ways – but I think it takes longer and is more work to do this on your own and it requires years of dedicated study and practice before you would be ready to begin.

A Curse

"It is better to light a candle than to curse the darkness." ~ Ancient Proverb

Tasha and I were back at home and everything was going very well. We liked our home, we got to travel to Peru once a year, we were chasing our dreams... We were still tight on cash but we always found ways to live life to the fullest and still chase our passion. I spent a lot of time researching mysticism and healing online and trying to share my own experiences in case others might learn from them, and as you may have experienced online before – sometimes debates can get a little heated....

While everything was going well for us and we generally felt like we had excellent luck – one day things suddenly shifted drastically. Tasha got along great with her employers and we got along great with our landlords, but suddenly for no reason – Tasha lost her job and we got kicked out of our house for seemingly no reason. We were confused because both of these things came out of nowhere and didn't really make any sense how they had happened. At the same time my work really slowed down. Pretty much everything that could go wrong started all going wrong at once, and even the weirdest things you would never expect to go wrong were all going wrong. A couple days later while moving our car broke down, all the people supposed to help us move had to bail, and while moving somehow a number of things were either broken or lost – we had moved many times before and never had these types of issues. Once we got into the new house everything started breaking – the sink, the shower, the toilet, the window.... It was the craziest string of bad luck – so we wondered if there was something causing this. It was just too many things all at once to be a coincidence.

So I went out to a local park with lots of woods and drank San Pedro by myself. I asked the medicine why we were having so much bad luck. Suddenly I saw a vision of someone I knew – a man I sometimes spoke to online. I remembered that the day before the string of bad luck started he and I had disagreed online and he had blown up about it. San Pedro told me he had used Enochian magic to curse me, but that I could fix things. Goes to show how immature some people who practice magic can be that someone would curse another person over a silly disagreement – I would have never considered it if San Pedro hadn't shown me his face. But in some ways – I wasn't that surprised considering some of his behavior in the past. I remembered another friend had claimed that this same character had curse him a couple months before and I hadn't thought twice about it, but this brought things into perspective.

Luckily I figured out what the issue really was and how to fix it! San Pedro told me not to send the energy back to him as many people do when removing curses. San Pedro told me to rise above. I was instructed to make an offering to the local spirits of the land near my new house and ask them for protection, as well as ask them to transmute the energy of the curse into positive energy. The idea was basically that this person had already sent me the energy, and now that it was mine I could do whatever I wanted with it. He attached a malevolent intent to the energy, but energy can always change forms, and he was no longer in charge of the energy he had sent to me. It was mine now and I could do whatever I wanted with it.

So I grabbed some materials that seemed good for the offering – some food, alcohol, sweets, seeds, and also some quick drawings I made of what I wanted to happen. I set down some wrapping paper, opened sacred space by calling in the directions, and then started making my offering. I prayed a lot. I prayed for the spirits to bless my offering, and each object I put into the offering I would first pour all my intentions and prayers into it and give it good energy, while also stating what that object symbolized to me and why I chose it for the offering. I made a mandala by placing all the objects with my intuition. As I finished I prayed over it one last time and then I buried it. I then stood up, smoked some mapacho and started singing – I danced and sang for 20 minutes just letting my intuition guide me and channeling the energy flowing through me like a hallow bone. As I finished the song I felt a huge energetic shift.

After that our luck shifted completely. Tasha found a new job that was much more fitting then the one before. Our new house was way better. My business picked up. Our car was fixed much cheaper than expected. All kinds of new opportunities came into our lives.

I also learned a valuable lesson from San Pedro about transmuting energy and taking the high road. I didn't have to play this game of sending the curse back to him, and then starting this back and forth endless battle. I thought about how in the Amazon the Ayahuasqueros always do this – they just curse each other back and forth and constantly have to defend themselves. They perpetuate the cycle. But by not sinking to the level of this person who had attempted to curse me I had not only stopped the cycle and moved on, I had also benefited greatly by using that negative energy to create something positive.

Smoke Meditation

When Tasha and I had looked for our new home in the last chapter we used a new ritual to find it. Since our first trip to Peru we had been building a relationship with mapacho. It was a bit difficult at first – neither of us were smokers and the mapacho is very strong. It is a different species of tobacco that is 11-18 times stronger than the common Virginia style tobacco most people smoke. After a couple small puffs we couldn't handle anymore – one single rolled cigarette of the mapacho would last us 4 different smoking sessions if we shared it! But in South America this was considered one of the most if not the most important plant for healing and ceremony. Ayahuasca and San Pedro shamans would both use it and there were even some healers called tobaqueros who specialized in using just tobacco to heal the sick. Their view of the plant was totally different then what we had grown up with in the modern world.

We saw the way tobacco was used in South America, and based on the effectiveness of their healing abilities we trusted that this plant did have healing potential when used correctly. In the jungle the shamans would ingest huge amounts of this extra strong tobacco and have no health issues – they smoked it, drank it, snorted it – sometimes at dosage levels that should be lethal, yet they were all super healthy. But we still had years of programming telling us tobacco was dangerous and harmful and we knew how deadly it was where we lived. Why was it so different in the Amazon? Our best guess was maybe it was the intention and respect. We live in a world of duality where there are harmful and beneficial energies, but the plant spirits live in a non-dualistic experience where they do not see things in terms of good or bad. Remember the lesson Ayahuasca had taught me about death healing all? The plants would help us if they could, but they weren't worried if we were never saved – because life would go on and we would be healed and find peace in death. So when you use tobacco with intention and ask only for its medicine then that is what you get. But if you use it habitually and unconsciously just to get a buzz then the plant just gives you what you asked for and doesn't worry about whether or not it is harmful for you. I think in many ways the same could be said of other plant use such as cannabis which can be a powerful medicine, or can be something that starts to take you over.

Tobacco is often described as an amplifier of intention or even as a direct line of communication to the spirits – so if you imagine that every time you light up that the whole spirit world is listening to your thoughts and feelings – maybe you can see why it is important to only use the plant with careful intention. When it is offered as a gift to the spirits it amplifies the expressed gratitude and when used along prayers it can amplify the power of those as well. Even if used habitually or unconsciously it might amplify things you don't want it to amplify, so here you might see where some of the danger lies. Imagine taking a smoke break at work and while you are smoking you are thinking about how stressed you are, how much you hate work, or how much someone bothered you – then imagine amplifying all that frustration or anger and how that might affect your body and mind. And since tobacco is a mild psychoactive that increases neuroplasticity it may also be strengthening whichever neural pathways are used during the smoking – so you could be strengthening these negative thought forms at the same time you smoke if you are unaware. Modern day smokers may be using tobacco to help them feel confident in social situations or to repress unwanted feelings or distract them from the moment – and there is a lot of information out there suggesting suppression may lower your immune system. This is very different for example from someone praying to tobacco for healing and protection, or using the plant to help them embrace and work through their feelings.

The mapacho on its own was a little strong for us at first, but we did start adding very small amounts of it to our cannabis and this was very nice. This was how we first started making our initial connection and relationship with mapacho. This also changed our relationship to cannabis in the best possible way. Because we wanted to respect the mapacho we started praying each time we would smoke this blend, and quickly we realized we should also be praying anytime we smoked cannabis. We never smoke any plant without praying to it first now.

Since we were praying with these plants we would also set an intention. Sometimes this intention would be as simple as asking the plant to bless and open our hearts. Sometimes we would ask for specific guidance – like in the case of wanting to find our new house.

When we were looking for a new house we ended up having two spots we needed to choose between. One spot was a great location for ceremony but was a small house and we would have neighbors close by. But we could walk straight into a giant park with beach and forest and tons of land to explore and do ceremony outdoors in. The other house was with some friends who would be fun to live with – they were into the same lifestyle as us and were musicians and gardeners who we would love to hang out with all the time. The house had a little more privacy but no access to nature close by. We were unsure which would be the best fit for us.

So we went out to a nice spot in nature and had a spliff of cannabis and mapacho blended together. We sat and prayed with this spliff for a while and thought about our intention. When we felt ready we lit it up and took just a few puffs, then put it out and laid back to close our eyes and journey. In some ways this is sort of like the core-shamanic style journey, but instead of a drum and going through a tunnel we were using the smoke to enter a trance, and then you "grab" onto the smoke with your consciousness and let it take you on the journey. So as the smoke took me on a journey I saw a hummingbird and this hummingbird showed me the house by the park right away – I knew that was where we needed to live. I opened my eyes and Tasha was opening her eyes at the same exact time.

I asked "So you saw the same house I did?" She nodded. "So we are going to move next to the park?" and she nodded again. We had seen the same house. As we left the forest we ended up going by the house and we both saw two hummingbirds circle around us and then land on top of the house. If that isn't a sign, I don't know what is!

I learned some other ways to use the smoke as well. I found I often got the best results while blending cannabis and mapacho together, but all of these methods can work with either plant on its own as well. A couple of things I do want to mention though – you want quality tobacco grown in the best way possible with no additives (even the "organic" brand American Spirits isn't organic and has added carcinogens), cannabis grown organically and with less nutrients added is best (cannabis can be grown with rich soil using worms and bugs to keep soil healthy rather than nutrients), and you don't need to smoke too much or over-do it! A little can go a long way, and smoking too much can leave you sick or stoned and make the process harder.

Most of my healing work is done in person but every once in a while I get a request from someone to do distance energy work. One day I decided to try this with the smoke first to see if it was more effective. I had set up a time for the client to relax somewhere quiet at home while I did the work and we had agreed I would be doing distance work using my Q'ero style altar as well as song and shamanic journey. So after I opened sacred space I smoked a little bit of mapacho with cannabis and I used that time and the smoke to help me enter a trance state as well as to start making an energetic connection with the person I was going to work on. I spent a few minutes really building that energetic connection to them. Once I felt thoroughly connected I went to my altar and started doing the style of energy work I do using the altar and singing. Afterwards I did a journey to get advice for them to help get the most benefit from the work we did. When I spoke to the client the next day it turned out that during the session we had both seen many of the same images, he had felt a lot of heat and movement in the area of his body that I ended up working on, and there was a noticeable improvement in their condition. The smoke isn't necessary for this type of work, but it did make it easier for me and more effective.

You can use the smoke in many different ways. Sometimes when I am confused about something or feel like I need insight on a subject or healing I will pray with my herbs and set my intention, light it up, then meditate afterwards and really go into my intuition and emotions on the topic. In this way you can really sensitize yourself and bring awareness and clarity to life's challenges. This is the difference between smoking a plant to numb yourself or smoking a plant to find healing – intention and where you direct your consciousness and attention can completely change the effect of the plant.

Working with tobacco within other ceremonies is also very helpful. The smoke can be used as a vehicle for the spirit of the plant and this spirit is known to be one of the best protectors and cleansers of energy. It is also a heart opening plant and can teach you about healing and magic. The smoke can be blown around a room or on a person to cleanse their energy or call in protection, and can be used on yourself in the same way. It can also be used to help focus your mind, give you an energy boost, help you connect with other spirits, or help you enter a trance. In almost every single situation it can be helpful. If you are pregnant or have a respiratory illness you should avoid it however – better safe than sorry.

Another helpful tip for working with tobacco is to set up rituals or specific patterns for how you use it. For example – pick a certain way to use it for protection and always do that when setting protection with tobacco. This is helpful because if you are too disoriented with another plant medicine or even just an intense emotional state then your body will naturally use the habitual pattern you have developed and that pattern will hold your intention. For example, in a mushroom ceremony I might get a little more disoriented then I meant to or have an intense moment where it is hard to focus – but if I always blow on someone's crown 3 times to protect them, then my body and the plant spirit will naturally use that pattern even if I am disoriented or distracted. Normally it is helpful to take a moment and focus on your intention while you are blowing the smoke, but in ceremonies sometimes things are challenging and need to get done and it can be helpful to have a pattern to follow back onto that still holds your intention. With tobacco in particular I think it is helpful to have a blowing pattern for cleansing and for protecting so that you can always do those two tasks well even if deep in the ceremony.

The Q'ero Style Mesa and the Chakana

During our second trip to Peru Tasha and I received our mesa altars from the Q'ero tribe and began learning how to work with them. We had some lessons from a Q'ero paqo, a couple books, and our intuition to guide us. Later that year I also met a lady who had spent years working with the Q'ero who lived in Seattle near us and taught shamanism classes at a local college. I met with her and became her teaching assistant at the college and also was able to learn a lot from her. Quickly our altars became a main staple of our personal practices and was our go-to medicine when we weren't using plants, or when we needed to support our plant work. To this day I consider my practice to be mostly based on working with plant medicines and my mesa – everything else is a side-note for me.

Mesa's are altars that come in many forms – most often a large table or blanket with a healers medicine items arranged across it in a grid or structure to invoke healing and wisdom. It is the motherboard that connects the healer to all the spirits and energies they need to help their community. The Q'ero mesa is a bit unique in that they also fold up into medicine bundles with all of the contents fitting inside, and this is usually how they are carried around and worked with. The healer does much of their work with the mesa closed, but also opens it up to work with depending on the situation. The outer cloth which holds the mesa together is called a mastana and is generally made of a beautiful and intricately woven cloth containing the woven geometric language of the Inka in its patterns. Inside the cloth are most importantly stones and crystals which connect the healer to the Apu's and mountain spirits, and also other items like herbs and plants, shells, pictures, symbols or figures like crosses or small staffs and keys. The bundle is then tied together with a symbolic string called the huaraca – which symbolically ties the healer to the Sun.

Everything in the mesa is based on symbolism to help remind the paqo (healer) about their connection to all of life around them. The woven symbols on the cloth might depict the condor or the puma, or Grandfather Sun or Mother Ocean. The stones inside connect the paqo to the mountain spirits, but they also represent the healers connection to the upper, middle and lower worlds that so many healers and shamans seem to work with. You can have any number of stones on your mesa and they can represent anything meaningful to you, but I chose to build my altar with 12 main stones in the completed mesa – 3 in each of the four directions to represent the 3 worlds in each direction. A 13th stone holds the center and traditionally this is a stone given to you by your teacher. I was taught to organize my mesa this specific way but I have seen others teach different associations. Each stone has its specialty and specific area of expertise, and these stones combined with the energy of the mesa is a large source of the paqo's expertise in healing. The four directions which the stones are associated with are depicted in the Andean medicine wheel which in some ways is very similar to the North American medicine wheel, but with different animals to represent the directions. This symbol of the medicine wheel is called the chakana and this symbol has been used in ancient temples of Peru for at least 3000 years if not longer.

Chakana means "to cross" or "to bridge" to the future, present and past. It represents these three levels as the serpent or past which is also the lower world, the puma is the present and middle world, and the condor is the future and upper world. The snake represent trials from your past and is a teacher. By learning from those trials you no longer have to repeat them and you can stop the cycle they perpetuated and leave them in the past with a simple thank you. The puma represents the present and our ability to support ourselves and be strong and live now. The condor represents the future where we are fully in our power and spirit and can create everything which our spirits desire.

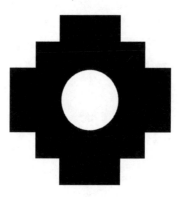

Besides the steps of the chakana representing the 3 worlds the symbol also represents the 4 directions similar to the medicine wheel. The Andean medicine wheel starts in the South with Amaru (or Sach'amama) – the great serpent. This is related to the element of Earth and also to the physical body. In the west is the great cat or Hatun Puma – either a jaguar, puma or black panther. West relates to water and the emotional body. Sitting in the North is the royal hummingbird Saiwa'kinti who teaches us about the heart and following your passion in life. North is associated with fire and soul purpose. The fourth direction East is held by the condor Kuntur or the great eagle Apuchin. This direction is where you find your vision and wisdom as well as your connection to the Upper World. All these directions are represented on the Chakana – the Andean Cross, which has 3 layers in each of the directions to represent the 3 worlds in each direction – just like the 12 stones in a mesa. The 12 stones can also represent the 12 most important Apu's that surround Cusco. In the center of the chakana is a circle which represents the naval or Qosqo/Cusco. This is represented in the mesa as a 13th stone which is traditionally given to you by your teacher.

So how can someone build their own mesa and experience this wisdom for themselves? You do not need any special materials, all you need is a personally significant cloth of some kind to be your mestana, 12 stones that specifically call out to be in your mesa and something nice to tie it all together with. You don't need to start with all 12 stones, but if it feels more appropriate you can build up to 12 over time as you connect with and grow your mesa. If you have anything else significant that wants to be in your mesa add that as well, because the stones like to be kept company and this is your medicine bundle – a reflection of you that should be personal and unique!

To fold your mesa correctly into the tied medicine bundle you start with the mesa laid out in a diamond shape in front of you. All of your medicine items should be in the center. First you fold the bottom corner up over the items – connecting the earth to the sky. Then you fold the right side next which is the masculine side associated with mysticism – fold the corner to the center of the mesa, and then fold the flat flap or side that is left on that side over the bulge of your medicine items within. Then you repeat the fold on the left side, which is the feminine side associated with magic and healing. After that you fold the top side down which is symbolically your head and there should be a perfect spot to tuck this flap into your mesa. Afterwards tie the mesa across the middle of the bundle with your string – tie it each direction to hold the bundle together so you can carry it without the contents spilling out. You now have your finished mesa!

To begin working with your mesa the best thing to do is to meditate with it, talk to it, carry it with you. Open it up often to handle the stones or set it up for special ceremonies or meditations at home. Whenever you open the mesa say a small prayer welcoming and thanking the spirits – thank Pachamama (Mother Earth), Creator and the Apus and your spirit guides. Eventually you will learn what each stone is for and what it specializes in, and eventually the mesa will teach you how to use it for healing and divination. If you use the stones for healing always clean them afterwards before they go back into your mesa, and when it feels appropriate it is also a good idea to feed your mesa – feed it some herbs or leaves which you might place in the bundle for a few days, feed it flowers or smoke from a sacred burning herb. Feed it with energy from a ceremonial fire. Feed it any way you feel called to. To clean the stones you can use any method you normally use for cleansing crystals – some options include smudging with tobacco or sage, holding the stone over a fire/candle to burn away Hucha, placing them on the Earth for Pachamama to clean, or letting them sit in running water ect...

Meditating with the mesa or doing energy work with the mesa is not based on following rules or copying someone else but is more based on your intuition. So you really want to practice the hollow bone technique we talked about earlier and just go with the flow. You will feel an urge to use a certain stone and place it here, or to do something with your hands or to sing a song. Trust your intuition. You may even receive visions or insights during the process – these should be shared and discussed in a responsible way after the session. If you see something really dark – for example maybe you feel like you pulled maggots out of their heart, you may wish to just say that you pulled some heavy energies out of their heart so that you do not scare or worry them too much. It is good to share, but be tactful about it.

When images or sensations appear they may come to you in different ways and sometimes this will tell you what kind of work you are doing with them. Maybe you get lots of sensations in your body or feel hot and cold places, or maybe the visions come from a low down perspective – this may mean you are working with snake energy and helping them heal the past or their body. Maybe you see lots of water or feel lots of emotions or memories coming up – this might be a clue that you are working from jaguar or puma. If you see lots of flowers, childlike images or very artistic images you may be working in hummingbird, and if you see eagles, rams, snow, mountain peaks or clouds you may be working in condor. These are just some clues. Even the stones you use during the session will give you clues – each stone has a specific purpose, so if someone chooses a stone you know heals sexual wounds and shame then there is a clue about what is causing their problem.

If you don't open up the mesa you can still use it in its bundled form as well – tap it on something or someone that you want to bless or send Sami to, or drag it along someone energy field to cleanse their Hucha. Keep trusting your intuition about what to do here.

The mesa is a great and personal tool that will grow with you as you grow. It is a reflection of you so treat it with honor, respect and love. Meditate with it and it will speak to you – listen and it will teach you. Always be grateful for what it offers, and when you hold that gratitude in your heart remember the Q'ero and their story of preserving this medicine to share with the rest of the world.

Beautiful and Challenging Ceremonies

"Look at the trees, look at the birds, look at the clouds, look at the stars... and if you have eyes you will be able to see that the whole existence is joyful. Everything is simply happy. Trees are happy for no reason; they are not going to become prime ministers or presidents and they are not going to become rich and they will never have any bank balance. Look at the flowers — for no reason. It is simply unbelievable how happy flowers are." ~ Osho

We had many ceremonies over the next couple years. We were taking people to Peru for retreats, hosting our own ceremonies, and doing a lot of personal study as well. Ceremonies are never the same and they never cease to surprise you no matter how many you have sat in. There is always more to heal and more to learn, and each person brings their own needs and personality to the ceremony that changes the experience as well.

I remember it took me about 3 years to heal my own depression, and some other people I saw in ceremonies had similar process's which took a lot of work and time to get through. But sometimes I saw people completely transform in a single ceremony like a true miracle from heaven. It was so exciting to see everyone's process and to witness the magic at hand. I remember one lady who healed migraines she had for over 15 years in a single mushroom ceremony, and another lady who healed frozen shoulder that had bothered her for 20 years in a single afternoon with San Pedro. Another friend was having 2-4 panic attacks every week but after one single drink of San Pedro and a ceremony with a lot of crying – she stopped having them completely overnight. These were all people I met before they found healing and I saw them heal before my eyes – not a story I read about or heard from someone, but something I got to see myself.

Some ceremonies even got a little scary for a while. I remember the first time I saw an exorcism. I was hosting San Pedro ceremony in Peru and Juan and Louis from the Q'ero tribe happened to be there helping out and giving cleansings with their condor feathers. I saw Louis work on one lady and I went to ask her how it was – she replied in a distressed tone: "I saw it and I want it gone! It has eyes and teeth and it's on my shoulder – get rid of it!" I asked her if she thought it was ready to come out and she didn't know, so I thought maybe it needed a second to get ready. I told her I was going to check on everyone real quick and then come back so I can focus all my attention on her, and that she should just try to get ready and let the medicine initiate the process.

As soon as I finished checking on everyone I heard a blood-curdling scream like someone was being murdered. I have never heard a scream like that in my life. I ran to see what was happening and she was screaming and flailing around – obviously in a lot of pain and probably very scared. I was scared myself – seemed like an intense spirit and who knew what would happen to me when I tried to help her? I was thinking I need to grab my mesa and my tobacco and all my tools but someone said, "I think she needs a hug." I decided to start with that.

I ran over and hugged her while she screamed. I prayed to every spirit I could think of to protect both of us and help us. I prayed and sent her all of the light and medicine that I could – and suddenly her screams turned into laughter, "It's gone! It's gone!" Everyone in the garden started laughing. I looked at her and she looked different – her facial features and skin tone had changed, her eyes had changed. Even her personality had changed. She was like a completely different person. That was the first time I had ever seen the medicine perform an exorcism, but it wasn't the last. I am glad the Q'ero paqo's were there for the first one though as they gave me a lot more confidence – I figured if I got messed up trying to help her that maybe the Q'ero brothers could save my ass!

Sometimes the ceremonies didn't just effect you while under the influence of the plants either. I mentioned the San Pedro ceremony with Lesley where I started seeing angels before I had even drank any medicine. I have another story as well with the mushrooms taking me into a two week long ceremony. The first time I have ever eaten mushrooms in nature was when I had gone backpacking for the first time. A went with a friend to the Olympic Hotsprings and we did a 6 mile hike and ate mushrooms one day. It was an amazing and insightful experience but for years I wasn't able to make it back there – at first I just didn't have my own backpacking gear but once I got my own gear the trail was closed for years for maintenance. Once it opened back up I really wanted to take Tasha there and share the experience with her so we planned a 3 day trip just the two of us. The first day we hiked into the hotsprings and set up camp. The next morning we woke up and had the hotsprings to ourselves so we did a ritual bath ceremony asking the waters to cleanse our energy. We finished in the hotsprings, ate some mushrooms and started our 6 mile hike that goes up to an alpine lake and then back down to camp.

I had been waiting about 5 years to repeat this hike so I was super excited. Early on in the hike the mushrooms told me something kind of strange – they said if I took off my glasses and did the whole hike without them that they would heal my eyesight. I was skeptical – I don't believe something just because someone tells me, and I don't necessarily believe the plants or fungus every time they tell me something…. But at the same time I didn't want to be too stubborn and miss an opportunity for healing because I wouldn't listen to the mushrooms. I am very blind without my glasses and I was so excited to see this hike again…. It kinda killed me a little inside but I decided to go for it. I didn't have my glasses case with me so I had to carry them in my hand the entire hike which was a hassle, and the mushrooms make the scenery look so amazing but I couldn't see anything without my glasses. The mushrooms told me I had to go the entire hike to the top of the mountain without putting on my glasses at all so I couldn't even sneak a quick look. I rushed our hike up the mountain because I wanted to wear my glasses and see so badly, so we didn't really take our time to enjoy ourselves as much as we normally would have.

While walking up the mountain and not being able to see I was reminded of some trauma from my childhood though. I remembered how it had taken me 2 years to get glasses after my eyesight got poor, so for a while I walked around all the time not being able to see. I couldn't recognize people's faces and I couldn't read the whiteboard in school – it is actually very scary walking through life and not being able to see properly. It always made me feel vulnerable. At one point I was so focused on my memories and walking up the mountain that I didn't even realize I was unconsciously putting the glasses back on my head – they were on before I realized I was doing it and I quickly took them back off. They were only on for a second and I didn't mean to put them on…. I hoped I hadn't just messed things up – but in a way I didn't even know if I trusted the mushrooms to heal my vision anyways.

We eventually made it to the top and I finally put on my glasses. I felt like I could relax for the first time on the hike. We played around the lake, meditated for a bit and had some time to enjoy the scenery. I was feeling pretty good the rest of the hike until we made it back down to camp. When we got to camp I started feeling frustrated that the mushrooms hadn't healed my vision and I wondered why they had lied to me…. They are sometimes trickster spirits, but I was still confused. I hated that I had missed so much of the hikes beauty since I had my glasses off and felt like the mushrooms had kind of screwed me over on that one. It also started raining really hard and got very cold out – I ended up a little wet so I couldn't wear all of my clothes in my sleeping bag and I was colder that night and had trouble sleeping. I woke up in a bad mood and just wanted to get off the mountain and go home at that point.

I was in a nasty funk for 2 weeks straight after that. Normally I am a pretty relaxed and happy person and I couldn't think of anything wrong that should be bringing me down, but I just felt horrible. I was angry, confused and felt lost. I hosted a couple ceremonies and while everything went well for everyone in the ceremony the medicine would only tell me how to support others and wouldn't talk to me about anything else. It wouldn't help me solve any of my own problems or help me search into my heart – it was very strange and unusual. I felt totally disconnected from all my spirit guides.

After 2 weeks of this I decided to step things up and I did a solo ceremony by myself with a large cup of San Pedro. A really large cup. I spent the day out in the forest and really focused on myself. I was still having trouble connecting so I just sat down and really prayed. I prayed with all my heart and really felt the desire within myself for that connection and clarity – and suddenly it all came. I saw what the mushrooms had done – they had pulled out all my insecurities and all the fears and lies I told myself and brought them to the surface so that I would be forced to experience them and see how false they were. I doubted myself as a healer and so I had to experience that doubt to see how false it was. I doubted the plants and my spirit guides – so I had to experience that doubt and disconnection to really see how real my guides were to me. I had to work through all these doubts and more, all the lies I was telling myself – as I lived them and experienced them I saw how false they were.

I was ecstatic. I saw that the mushroom trip which I had thought put me into a two week funk was actually one of the most insightful and empowering ceremonies I had had yet. I felt myself growing and as soon as I went back to my practice it was much deeper. I faced my shadow and worked through my doubts and in the process learned how to be more of myself – how to express more of myself. That struggle became a lesson and a triumph and a great gift.

Sometimes the medicine will start to change things in the world around you or orchestrate strange coincidences that seem impossible. This especially seems true of the Amanita Muscaria mushroom. When I first started working with this mushroom I would smoke the skin off the top of the mushroom – it has a light and mild dreamy effect that sometimes surprises you in ways you wouldn't expect. One time Tasha and I smoked this in the woods at a park in Seattle. The mushroom is legal in USA and we had picked this one growing wild in the same park a couple weeks before. As I lit up the first joint of this mushroom a giant raven flew up to us. Ravens do not like cities and this is the only time in my life I ever saw one in a city – and interestingly enough ravens are an omen that supposedly marks entering the spirit world from the ordinary world, so this was interesting timing.

I had a flute in my pocket made from a condor bone and I started to play a little music on it – the raven started mimicking what I was playing! I would play something and then the raven would sing it back perfectly. After a while it just seemed too crazy so we started walking off and for the next 20 minutes the raven would follow us mimicking the last phrase I had played on the flute over and over. As the raven finally left a squirrel came up and looked at us with a glimmer in its eye. For some reason there was a cashew in my pocket so I bent over and held it out in my hand for the squirrel as a kind of joke. The squirrel ran around me three times and then jumped onto me and ate the nut out of my hand before running off! I had never experienced anything like this before and I was blown away. The rest of the day I carried another cashew in my pocket and every time I stuck my hand in my pocket and felt the cashew I would get so excited hoping another squirrel would come by. No more squirrels came up to me, but the cashew taught me a powerful lesson that day about enjoying the moment and the little things in life, and I ended up putting that cashew in my mesa and carrying it for over a year there because of how much it touched me that day. We also had powerful experiences with some other animals that day – 2 bald eagles seemed to be playing with us and we saw a pod of orcas playing off the beach which I have also never seen in the city before.

Another time Tasha and I decided to do an Amanita ceremony around death and abandonment – this was related to healing some grief from my mother's suicide. We had a favorite park we wanted to do the ceremony at and the day before the ceremony we were at the same park talking about how we would do ceremony the next day. The park was normal. But one day later when we showed up for ceremony the park had completely changed overnight – there were hundreds of dead salmon all over the place with all of their bellies sliced open and eggs spilled out and all their eyes missing. For a month afterwards the whole park stank like dead fish. I still go to that park all the time and make a special note to return to the park around that same time of the year – I have never found anything like it sense, and even if I missed the fish by a couple days there has never been that lasting stink like there was when we found all the dead fish. The timing of this message from nature could not have been more perfect.

Sometimes the plants give you a light and gentle ceremony, sometimes you feel like your entire life just changes in the space of a single moment. Sometimes you just feel a shift in perspective but nothing mystical, and sometimes you end up talking to spirits or becoming one with God. With all these miraculous healings and impossible coincidences working with the plants never gets old and no two ceremonies are ever the same.

Nature Mandala and Fire Ceremony

Here are two great ways to connect with nature no matter where you are. These rituals are tangible tools to help you honor transitions and cycles of life, open ways for shifts to occur in your life and being and to call forth balance and wholeness. We will start first with how to make a nature mandala as a ceremony for healing.

To start your nature mandala go for a walk in nature by yourself. It is a good idea to offer a prayer before you start walking and set an intention for your mandala – maybe something you want to heal or gain insight about. If you want to do a group mandala that is also possible following the same instructions but with a group, but I will discuss the process as if it is just one person. As you are walking let your intuition guide your feet. As you are walking you may feel called to gather some of the items you pass – a branch or a pine cone for example. Eventually you will come to a spot that feels right – don't rush the process but really let your feelings speak to you so you can come to the best spot for this ritual. This is your intuition picking up on the energies around you to guide you. As you find a spot that feels right look around for the exact place you will build your nature mandala. Then start gathering any other close by materials that speak out to you – all the materials you gather will be used to make your nature mandala. You can use anything you find – branches, leaves, pine cones, rocks, flowers, pieces of bark or anything else.

Once you have gathered what you feel is appropriate you can start making the mandala. Keep your intention in mind as you make the mandala and also let your intuition and feelings guide you as you arrange all the materials you gathered into an artistic shape and pattern or expression of what you feel inside. You can arrange the materials in any way you like – there are no rules and this is a pure expression of your feelings and intuition. The more you let go and really get into the feeling of this the better your results – you are being a vessel for spirit to work through in this creation.

When you feel like you are finished with the mandala take a moment to sit and connect with it. Meditate by it if you like, or feel free to pray or sing a song. If any emotions want to come out just let them flow. As you finish this take a moment before you leave to either take a picture of the mandala or look over and take a mental image for later. Try and remember what things looked like and maybe even think about if the placement of certain materials means anything to you personally.

The next day if you can return to your mandala. If you cannot return to it that is fine and the ritual can be complete with just the making of it and the prayer involved, but returning to the mandala the next day can sometimes be insightful. Look over the mandala you made and see if anything has moved or changed while you were gone. Listen to your intuition to see if those changes or lack of changes mean anything to you. You can also take a moment to pray more or express gratitude to the spirits who worked through your mandala.

Fire ceremony can be done indoors or outdoors. There are many ways to do fire ceremony so here is one simple method that you can use as inspiration. First off – when you gather your materials for the fire be present and mindful. Don't throw don't the wood but place it nicely. Stack it rather than leaving it in a messy pile. The entire process of gathering and building the fire should be done mindfully and thoughtfully.

It is also nice before coming to the fire to create or find an offering made out of natural burnable material – this can be a stick or a pine cone, or grass or flowers or even something more traditional like cedar. You can even have more than one offering if you like. The offering can either symbolize your gratitude to the fire spirit or it can represent something you want to let go of – sometimes it is nice to have an offering to represent both.

Prepare the fire. Begin by placing the kindling in the form of an equal armed cross to represent the 4 directions. You can then build a teepee of sticks and logs around this for the fire. You can also open sacred space at this time and call in the directions – ask the spirits as well as Grandfather Fire to bless your fire and your ceremony. After this you can ignite the fire. If you like you can use oils, wax or crumpled paper as an accelerant. Paper should be blank with no writing to respect the integrity of the ceremony and the fire. As the fire grows you can feed it with oil or with offerings of gratitude or both – when using oil I like to feed it three times. Sometimes it is nice to offer the oil first to the four directions or you can offer tobacco or cedar to the four directions of the fire, then make the offering again to the sky and earth, and then lastly as an offering to all the participants.

Observe the condition of the fire and watch for its readiness. Once the fire reaches maturity and readiness it will change color and burns in a different way. Almost like the fire has become sweet or mature. This is when the fire is ready for more ceremonial work.

This is a good time to bring your offerings. Bring the offerings in thoughtfully – for example you may wish to take turns approaching the fire from each of the four directions and then kneel at the fire and blow your prayers and intentions into the offering before placing it thoughtfully in the fire. You can also feed yourself from the energy of the fire – place your hands over the fire and gather in the energy radiating from it. Bring that energy first into your stomach, then your heart and then your forehead. If you have a mesa bundle you can also feed it with the energy from your sacred fire. Some people may wish to feed themselves from the fire as they place offerings and some people may wish to feed themselves after all offerings have been placed – the group should pick one of these and stick to it together. Watch your offerings burn in the fire and see them carry your prayers to the heavens with their smoke. Sometimes it is also nice for someone to stand behind you while you make an offering and to hold space for you while you are at the fire – consider if your group would like to do this.

Next if you like it is nice to make a group offering to Mother Nature or Pachamama – grab one large stick to represent this and pass it around so that all participants can give their dreams and blessing for the earth to this stick using their breath. Once this stick has been passed around and blessed by everyone the youngest and oldest person present can hold the stick together and offer it to the fire as one.

Now you can call the ancestors to the fire. The whole group can pray and ask their ancestors to visit this fire and bless the fire and those around it. Hold space together and receive the ancestors. After this people can pray or just sit and watch the fire. It is nice to have a good time for meditation and prayer here so that everyone can receive wisdom from the fire. Let the burning and the smoke speak to you.

After everyone has had time to pray and meditate you may also wish to share experiences around the fire, or to share some sacred songs together or tell a sacred story. When this is done you can close sacred space. Usually two people should stay with the fire to make sure all offerings have burned and make sure the fire dies down to embers. When the fire has died down enough you can decide if it is okay to let it lie and fully die out on its own or if you need to cover it with water and sand to make sure it is completely out (always use fire safely and don't leave a unattended fire burning).

Creating A Stone Medicine Wheel

This is another ritual you can do anywhere in nature and with any purpose or intention. It is especially good for bringing concentrated areas of blessing and prayers to the land. It is also very helpful when you feel like you need the blessings of the 4 directions in your life or if you want to connect more deeply with those energies on a personal level. The process of creating the medicine wheel is generally very simple, but what makes it powerful is really spending a lot of time with your prayers while you make it, and putting the time and energy to make it as beautiful as you know how – really pour your love and care into the project.

A medicine wheel is a representation of the four directions and the center. Some can be very simple and small while others can be very complex and large. The most simple form of medicine wheel you can make is 5 stones. The medicine wheel can really take on almost any form as long as the center and 4 directions are clearly displayed, but a popular and beautiful design I like to use often is to have a circle with a cross intersecting the middle – all made of stones. The form is not the most important consideration though – it is really your prayers and intent that matters the most.

It is great if when making the medicine wheel you have some understanding of the 4 directions and what they mean to you. We discussed one way of understanding these directions earlier in this book – I use the Andean associations for the directions in my own rituals. You can feel free to use the Andean understanding of the directions as explained in this book or feel free to use any other system of understanding the 4 direction that makes sense to you. While it helps to understand the directions, even without those teachings the medicine wheel can be used to bring balance and blessings to the land.

You can do any opening ceremony you like before beginning, or just start with a simple prayer. Do what feels right to you and whatever best fits the moment. When you are ready to construct the medicine wheel first give yourself a smudge (any plant you like). Then find your stones – ask them to help you and give them an offering in gratitude. Make sure you at least have 5 stones to represent the four directions and center. Then smudge the stones as well.

Next find the piece of land where you will make the medicine wheel. Pray to the land here and then smudge this area as well. Talk to the spirit of the land and tell it your intentions to build the medicine wheel here. Give an offering of some kind – this can be tobacco, corn, milk ect… Place the offering right where the center of your medicine wheel will go.

Put down the center stone on the spot with prayers for balance and a strong connection to the center of all that is – the heart of creation. It is also an option to use a Y shaped stick here instead of a stone because in this tradition represents the balance of all things (like yin and yang). Remember – the most important focus here are your prayers.

Then step out of the circle area of the medicine wheel and face South. Hold your stone and make prayers for the Winds of the South and the Spirits of the South to come to this circle for all of your relations and to bring beauty, balance, peace and healing to this place. Put a small offering on the ground and place the stone on top of it. Now traveling clockwise around the center point repeat this process for the West, North and East. Once you are done you can fill in between the South, West, North and East stones with smaller stones to make a circle. You can also use smaller stones to make a larger cross within the circle.

Your medicine wheel is complete. It is good to take a moment to let the feeling of its completion sink in and to pray a little more. You can then leave the medicine wheel as an offering to the earth and the place it is built, or you can also sit and work with it more by asking questions and receiving answers from nature all around the wheel. Always travel clockwise when working with the medicine wheel.

Remember that making the medicine wheel is all about prayer. Pray to the four winds, the sky powers and the earth mother. Your prayers and intentions go into the stone people – they will remember them.

Teachers, Mentors and Lessons

"It is the supreme art of the teacher to awaken joy in creative expression and knowledge." ~ Albert Einstein

Throughout the years Tasha and I had many teachers or people who inspired us and influenced our own practices. We met many teachers in Peru, took classes in core shamanism or energy healing, found a teacher to help us connect with our mesa's, and I even became good friends with a couple local Ayahuasquero's practicing in Seattle who started teaching me. At one point I even began to assist one of these Ayahuasquero's for a couple years and did a couple diets with him – I learned a lot sitting so often with the medicine and watching other healers work. And of course we learned a lot on our own as we were always doing our own ceremonies and learning through experience directly from the spirits themselves. I think we really benefited a lot from having both perspectives of learning from others and also learning on our own – I think it is really hard or maybe even near impossible to learn everything on your own without inspiration from more experienced healers, but I also think you get stuck in a small box and miss out on a lot if you never experiment on your own as well. Learning in both ways really balances out the practice.

Being a practitioner is very different then what most people probably imagine. I remember when I first went to the Amazon to drink Ayahuasca I assumed that the shamans were so deep into their practice that they probably never got sick anymore and that was why they were so functional in ceremony. Little did I know at the time – they actually get just as sick as a lot of other people but just learned how to push through that and keep a level head even when the medicine is super strong or making them sick. Many times when practitioners sing to people in ceremony whatever they are cleaning off of people will actually attack the practitioner and make them sick – so they aren't just dealing with their own energies, but everyone else's energies are also affecting them and making them sick! I have had people sit down in front of me so I can sing to them and as soon as they sit down there energy will block my medicine or make me sick – it gives me a big clue what kind of work they need actually. In other cases when there have been nasty spirits that people bring into ceremony with them, that spirit will try and attack me when I attempt to remove it from the person, so then I have to defend myself at the same time that I am cleaning them.

You also pick up a lot of baggage left over from people. As a practitioner you are basically asking people to come and unload their baggage – so they tell you all their problems, unload their emotions on you, purge their energy on you…. And this is exactly what you want in some ways. You want them to let go and share their troubles with you so that you can help them. But some of this inadvertently will cling to you so you also spend a lot of time cleaning yourself and your house during and after ceremony. Luckily in the process of becoming a practitioner you develop a lot of skills to help you work through baggage so while it is a lot of work it doesn't hold you back as much as it could. But for a practitioner the ceremony is only part of the work – there is a lot of preparation before the ceremony and also a lot of cleanup afterwards. Sometimes it can takes weeks after a ceremony to fully process all the energy people left at your house, and in that time you might be doing more ceremonies so it can keep building up and feeling like a endless process of always trying to clean your house.

It can also be a little tough on the mind and body to do so many ceremonies. If you participate in the ceremony and also drink medicine with the people who come to see you then it is possible to end up doing 2-4+ ceremonies every week. The medicine is healthy for your body, but sometimes it is hard to sleep, or sometimes it is just exhausting always being in altered states. It can take a lot out of you to always be working through other people's energies. There are also some mundane tasks you also don't want to do in altered states – like drive to the grocery store. So sometimes these daily tasks and chores really start to pile up if you are hosting day long ceremonies regularly.

At the same time the work is very rewarding. You get to help a lot of people. You build a deep relationship with yourself and with the spirits. You see miracles. You connect with very interesting people in a very personal way. You get challenged in a positive way that helps you grow as a person. It is a beautiful thing.

Sometimes the saddest part of this life is watching people give up or hold themselves back…. People will ask for ceremonies then get scared and cancel at the last second. The medicine will offer someone a chance to heal and they will be too scared and turn it down. In a lot of cases people will choose a familiar discomfort or sickness to an unfamiliar empowered life. What is unfamiliar can be scary, and while people don't like being sick or depressed sometimes people are so used to it and comfortable with it that they prefer it to change.

I know I wouldn't be where I am without all my teachers and without the community that supports me. I remember the second time I went to the jungle Ayahuasca told me she wasn't my medicine – Tasha was my medicine. Relationships can be powerful medicine and a great tool for personal insight and growth if you pay attention and honor your relationships with all of your being. Nobody can walk this path alone – besides the spirits who work through us we all need community to support us in the long run.

I noticed that as a man I was taught in society to protect myself a lot. To be strong and dependable. This made me create a lot of walls and defenses. In some ways these walls were helpful – they protected me in ceremony and I wasn't usually too effected by other peoples energy that I might pick up. In other ways though I had to learn how to break down these walls and be more sensitive. I needed to do this so I could have deeper heartfelt connections with people and so I could sense energies more accurately. Sometimes I would even pick up energy and not notice it for a while because I had so many defenses – and that isn't really a good thing. I needed to be more aware of the subtle energies affecting me and the ceremony I was hosting. So for many years I worked on being more sensitive.

Part of becoming more sensitive is just doing more ceremonies – working with the plants, singing icaros, or doing mesa altar work. Part of it is also healing and cleaning yourself. A good example of how cleaning helps might be to imagine driving down a freeway with a dirty window. If another bug hits the window you don't even notice because the window is so dirty. But if you clean the window and it is spotless you notice every single little thing that hits the window. So cleaning and personal healing help a lot. What might have helped me the most though was dieting plants. I dieted plants in Peru, I found local healers to open diets for me, and I also opened my own diets. Opening your own diet is a little hard – you don't have anyone to introduce you to the plant so you are really on your own, but it does work.

As I became more and more sensitive I was able to sense and understand a lot more subtle energies – but I also lost some of my defenses in the process and this meant I had to learn better protection that didn't ruin my sensitivity. Part of this was learned through practice and doing more ceremonies – for example if someone needs help in ceremony and I sing to them, but there energy tries to jump to me and I defend myself, well I am gaining experience here. But what really helped the most again was dieting more protective plants. Dieting is an incredibly beneficial practice and really helps a ton. Some good protective plants might include Ajo Sacha, Mucura, Juniper, Cedar, Ayahuma, Mapacho, Blackberry ect... Through dieting I really learned how to be more sensitive as well as more protected, I learned more about healing, and I also got to work on myself and develop my own character. Dieting requires a lot of discipline and this is very good for your character.

The more you work with healing and plant medicines and the more you connect with nature and the world around you, the more you realize how everything in life can be a teacher and a medicine if you engage it in the right way. Struggle and challenges can be medicine, relationships can be medicine, chasing your dreams can be medicine, expressing yourself, observing others, observing nature, making art, connecting with community, time alone – all of these things can teach you and help you heal. Life is the greatest ceremony you can participate in.

At one point I felt a calling to connect with my tarot cards again. Tarot had been one of the first if not the first spiritual tool I had started to learn many years before, and while I still did readings sometimes it had been a while since I had deepened my study with them. So I decided to do a ritual asking the spirits of the Major Arcanum to connect with me and teach me. I decided to connect with each card for a week – almost like 22 one week dieta's but with archetypes instead of plants. So I made an altar for the working and each week I would have a card out on the altar that I was connecting with – each day I would take a moment to hold and look at the card while asking to connect with it, and once during each week I would do a more immersive ritual where I would call the spirit of the card to appear in my mind's eye and show me something.

I was completely blown away by the power in the cards and how they affected my life. Tasha wasn't even doing the working but the cards started affecting her too. They did not go easy on us. Too much happened to go into the details of what every card manifested in our lives, so I will share the most intense part of this working.

Around this time Tasha and I were talking about having a child at some point soon, but then a little trouble came up and we actually almost split up. We ended up attending an Ayahuasca ceremony hosted by some friends of ours to see if we could fix things in our relationship and in the second ceremony everything made sense – we realized the trouble in our relationship was a type of purging that needed to happen – letting go of some doubts and confusion, and afterwards we felt closer than ever. That night after ceremony Tasha surprised me by putting on her wedding dress and we decided right then that we wanted to start our family – we conceived that night.

We had always thought that we would have a San Pedro baby and were surprised that this was going to be an Ayahuasca baby. But we were so happy. We felt closer than ever in our relationship and we were both so excited to have a baby together. During this week of conception we were working on the Empress tarot card which has to do with fertility and birth. I found out about the baby and the pregnancy during the Lovers card.

Then we made it up to the Death tarot card. And we lost the baby. This was 13 weeks after conceiving and was the day before we planned on telling our extended families. We had just told our parents the day before. It was a very scary experience – Tasha woke up late in the night with horrible cramps and bleeding and really lost a lot of blood – I was very scared when I saw all the blood and it was a heartbreaking night. I saw my baby dying and worried about my wife's health with all the blood loss. Eventually we had to take her to the hospital and she had to have an operation because her body was having trouble passing the miscarriage on its own – the doctors said when they put her under she started singing in some language they didn't understand and sang through the whole operation. They had never seen anything like it before. We both knew she was singing medicine songs to protect herself even in her almost unconscious state.

Tasha and I were devastated. The miscarriage hit us both really hard and we were so sad to lose our child. In time we started to see this as a lesson from Ayahuasca – to show us how much we wanted to have children, to help us deeply appreciate any children we did have, and to help prepare us for when we would finally have children one day. It was a horrible experience, but in many ways we were grateful. And while the miscarriage and pain did bring a little friction into our relationship in the end it helped us build a much stronger bond and deeper understanding and appreciation for each other.

Family in Peru

"Nature does not hurry, yet everything is accomplished." ~ Lao Tzu

During our 4th trip to Peru Tasha and I had a very special surprise. My father and new step-mother decided to join our yearly retreat to Peru and drink medicine with us. This was something I had been dreaming of for about 10 years – ever since I first experienced union with the divine during a psychedelic experience. I always felt that one day I really needed to show this side of reality to my family and share this part of my life with them. My father had met our teacher Lesley during our wedding 2 years before and since then had been somewhat curious about plant medicines. Around the same time our families noticed how much we had changed since beginning our work with plant medicines and visiting Peru and would comment on how happy we seemed. My dad didn't feel like he had any serious issues to work on, but he felt like the plant medicines could probably help him in some ways and he knew there was probably a lot of his childhood that he could let go of.

So my family sat in 2 San Pedro ceremonies at Lesley's with us and were incredibly moved both times. They told me that they let go of so much and started seeing things from a completely new perspective. They also saw Tasha and me in action and in our element – and found a new understanding for who we are and what we do. It was an incredible time for me to be able to share the most profound aspect of my life with them finally. I learned so much during that retreat.

I had some deeply personal talks with my family and really learned a lot from my dad. He had a crazy 2 years leading up to the retreat and had changed a lot – I felt like he was a wiser and happier person then I had ever seen him be before. We talked a lot and I learned a lot from him. I also learned a lot just being able to share my work and my true self with my family – there is a side of me that people only get to see in ceremony and so far my family had never experienced that part of my life before.

We also connected a lot more with Lesley and her two sons Mark and Simon. In many ways they feel like my second family or my extended family and whenever I visit them I feel like I am returning home. We got married in Lesley's garden and we have so many memories with their family. This year when I watched Lesley I noticed she has so much power in her words. While other healers need to sing songs, do energy work and blow tobacco smoke – she only needs to talk to you and the love in your voice and in her being opens people's hearts to the miracles of San Pedro. I don't know if I have ever seen such a gifted healer or someone who embodies love so perfectly.

This was about four months after our miscarriage and we had decided that we wanted to try again for a child at Lesley's house. Before the rest of the group arrived for our retreat we did a ceremony with San Pedro asking to have a healthy baby – and we conceived again that night at Lesley's house where we had been married two years before. Right next to Temple of the Moon and with the medicine of San Pedro in us we started our family.

As the group arrived we told them that we were trying to conceive and have a healthy baby this retreat so when we did a despatcho offering with the Q'ero tribe everyone helped us by putting in prayers for us to have a healthy baby. It was how we always dreamed of starting our family and it felt so good to have my father there with us during this time. We felt surrounded by friends and family and medicine.

We also spent some time with Kush – a wonderful Ayahuasquero who had been drinking Ayahuasca for 46 years at that time and who we had met the year before. Tasha sat in an Ayahuasca ceremony with our child in her belly just beginning to form and while she didn't drink Kush and his wife sang to her and she said she had a full blown Ayahuasca experience without even drinking! She is super sensitive to energy and really appreciated this time to connect with our child so early in her pregnancy.

Coming home from Peru with this gift of a healthy child growing in Tasha's womb was the greatest gift we could ever imagine. We felt so blessed for the moments that guided us towards this life and so blessed to have this connection to the spirits of nature and the deep medicine that inspires us to chase our dreams. Nothing is more natural then creating and nurturing life.

The following months we spent so much time in gratitude for all the gifts and teachings we have found by connecting to nature. We spent a lot of time thinking about how we can help our child develop this same connection and appreciation. As we get nearer and nearer to the due date of our daughter our hearts swell more and more with the life force growing inside of Tasha. I still cannot believe the miracle of life that women sacrifice so much to manifest in our world. As Tasha carried the manifestation of our love that is our baby I appreciated her more and more on deeper levels then I ever knew imaginable.

We now prepare ourselves for our greatest medicine journey – welcoming our daughter to the world. Cedar Rose Bodick is due to arrive this week and we couldn't be more excited!

Nature Is Medicine

"You do not have to be good. You do not have to walk on your knees for a hundred miles through the desert, repenting. You only have to let the soft animal of your body love what it loves. Tell me about despair, yours, and I will tell you mine.

Meanwhile the world goes on.

Meanwhile the sun and the clear pebbles of the rain are moving across the landscapes, over the prairies and the deep trees, the mountains and the rivers. Meanwhile the wild geese, high in the clean blue air, are heading home again.

Whoever you are, no matter how lonely, the world offers itself to your imagination, calls to you like the wild geese, harsh and exciting – over and over announcing your place in the family of things." ~ Mary Oliver

There are so many ways to connect with nature. I know the things I have learned and experienced are only the tip of the iceberg. When I see the shamans of Peru working their magic I see true masters of the work who are years beyond my abilities and understanding – and even they claim they only have the tiniest bit of nature's magic to share.

I wish I could share more with you, but I hope that this is a good start. One of the beautiful things about life is that we all find out own path and journey to our medicine and we all discover our own wisdom from the world around us. Others can help get us started, maybe inspire us or point us in a good direction – but eventually we have to find and create our own paths through the forest to find our own truths. We each have a unique story and wisdom to share with the world and it is something that only we ourselves can find and express.

Life can be confusing and difficult sometimes. It is easy to lose sight of our path and I have gotten lost on my own path many times... But time and time again nature has always redirected me to where I need to go and what I need to see. It has always shown me the path back to my heart and back to Spirit. When I feel lost and confused I often turn to nature for clarity – and I know that nature can provide the same solace for you that it always has for me.

About the Author

Travis Bodick is an author, musician and ceremonial guide. All of Travis's books are written to help the reader engage with and encounter their own truth through direct experience. Travis especially focuses on nature based spiritual healing practices and helping clients encounter and know their own heart and soul. Helping others to find and embrace their true passion in life is Travis's greatest joy.

You can find Travis and his other books at SoulRemedy.org

How The Earth Saved My Soul is both a story and a nature based system of healing and self-discovery. While drowning in the ocean Travis was saved from death by a mysterious spirit and experienced visions that forever changed the course of his life. Trying to make sense of this experience he found himself on a spiritual quest of self-discovery that started with meditation, psychedelics and occult mystery schools and eventually led him to indigenous shamans of the Amazon and Andes of Peru.

The Plant Remedy details everything the reader needs to know to work with plant medicines safely and to contact the spirits of plants for guidance and healing. The methods in this book are a combination of traditional South American curanderismo and the authors own methods learned through trial and error, or straight from the spirits themselves. This book is a must have for anyone interested in plant spirits and plant medicines!

Creating the Universe is Travis's first title and focuses heavily on guiding the reader through the process of creating their own personal spiritual practice which can be as unique as each individual reader. It focuses on different styles of ritual and ceremony, and looks at the underlying mechanics of how magic and energy work.

Experience. Create. LOVE. takes everything from Creating the Universe a step further - especially focusing on practice over philosophy. The book follows the arrangement of the Kabbalistic Tree of Life, and by following the exercises in the book, the reader experiences and travels the entire Tree of Life starting at the Kingdom, and ending with the Crown. This book is a perfect example of the type of practice which can be created using methods and philosophy from Creating the Universe.

The Shadow Twin takes the reader down a new road and into the realm of fiction. This book is based on a dream Travis had in Peru after San Pedro ceremony at the Temple of the Moon, and is a direct communication from the cactus spirit. The story follows the adventures of a young boy encountering spirits and ghosts and his own conscience as he finds his own spirit guide - the Shadow Twin!

Made in the USA
San Bernardino, CA
07 December 2018